Gypsies Greed & Politics

Leonard D.Lindquist

AuthorHouse™
1663 Liberty Drive, Suite 200
Bloomington, IN 47403
www.authorhouse.com
Phone: 1-800-839-8640

First published by AuthorHouse 7/19/2007

ISBN: 978-1-4343-2350-7 (sc)
ISBN: 978-1-4343-2353-8 (hc)

Library of Congress Control Number: 2007904858

Printed in the United States of America
Bloomington, Indiana

This book is printed on acid-free paper.

Illustration by Shannon Palmer

Gypsies, Greed & Politics
May 8, 8:00 p.m.

Orientation: listen to the management talk about what is to be expected: fifteen minutes. union introduces itself: ten minutes. Walk the floor with all new hires—approximately forty-five of us. Go back to room and wait for assignment. Start time 9:42 p.m. Union takes us out to meet the boss. Meet boss; boss looks at you and puts you where he thinks you might have a chance to learn. Work with older worker for about one hour, then older worker says "it's all yours." Parts coming from another station. Oops! Miss that one. What have I gotten myself into? Finally figure it out. It's break time. Older worker who was training me picks up parts that I did not finish during break. Break is twenty-four minutes. Lots of people talking about new hires. Back on the job and fall behind again; older worker takes over and shows me trick to job. Lunch time—2:30 a.m. Getting tired, but have half the night to go. Older worker says "its' all yours." Working hard, but just don't have the system down. Arms hurt, hands hurt. Went through three pairs of gloves. Final break. Older worker says, "We're usually done by now, so I'll take over; just watch." He was very good at the job. Spring winder I think they called it. Job done in ten minutes. Job setter bought me a coke. Said, "You've got to get faster." I'm in shock, but tomorrow I will try harder.

May 9, 9:30 p.m.

Report early. Ready to work the job I learned last night, but someone is not there. Boss says, "Take another person's job." I do. Parts pile up. I work through break to catch up. Boss watches me work through break and then, when the line starts, up the job setter steps in and says, "Take a break." I do. Take ten minutes go to the restroom and get some water. Hurry back. Job setter shows me trick to job. I learn it and become better. Never had a chance to look around until after we were done on the line. This plant is huge. Not used to working third shift, and can't sleep during the day.

Ninety days—milestone—I got in. Benees, raises, part of the group. Whatever that means. Of the forty-five of us, I think only a few didn't make it. Reasons unknown, but more than likely it was a shock to the system. They just didn't show up. I work in department three. I've worked nine hours a day for six weeks, including two Saturdays and Friday nights. Third-shift people are different. What I mean is that when it's morning for everyone it's afternoon or night for them. Let's go to the Shanty Lounge. They work at 7:00 a.m. One Friday morning I did. They cashed my check. Enough said. Had to work that Friday night. Slept all day. Learned that I could put in for different jobs. Kind of scared, but do. Put in for Henry and Wright job, which is a press run by an operator. Meet lots of people. Through group. Three days or you're done. Go back to department three. Too much pressure. I did try it again later and made it. Making lots of money. Need a new car. Buy a 1978 Chevy Camaro—beautiful. One of the prettiest cars I ever owned. Learn to call union rep when boss is being mean. Get into trouble with boss; clocking in late according to him, even though I'm on time. Penalty coming. Shop committee man Bob Olivarez called down. The rest is for the record books. Six months later, foreman is transferred. I got paid for time off. Eventually that boss is let go.

Decide to go on first shift. Play softball for the Local 326. Orange uniforms. Lots of fun. Worked in different departments: eight, nine, and one. Really liked nine, which was seatbelts. We were the only manufacturer of seatbelts for GM. We did a great job. Not that much overtime, but the quality was there. Our price apparently was too high, and GM eventually gave the seatbelts to an outside supplier. Fisher Body was great to work for; however, they didn't anticipate anything and were caught off guard. We had what we called temporary layoffs for six weeks at a time. Rotation. Worked well for a while. Eventually I got laid off—permanently! Ouch. October 1981: Reagonomics set in. Actually, President Reagan hadn't put his budget to work yet. It was the aftermath of Carter and the debacle of the Iran hostage affair. Gas, which was only sixty-nine cents a gallon in 1976, had almost doubled to $1.19 per gallon in 1981. What an impact. Learn what a subcheck and subcredits really are as the union subfund dwindles fast and they start taking five credits for one check. I didn't figure on that. Get a job. Sell cars. Who's going to buy them? Pay for own insurance during layoff though COBRA—$256 per month. Wife is expecting. GM comes out with Citation, Omega, and Ventura. Engineering at it's poorest. No wonder I don't have a job. But wait! June 1983: GM wants me back. Okay, I'll go back. Nothing has changed. Same work at Fisher Body. They didn't get into plastics like they should have. Products are not good. Survive till fall of 1984. Cars aren't selling. Get laid off. Get picked up by V-8 plant. Nobody wants those Citations, etc.

Build V-8s for Cutlass, Grand Prix, Riviera, Eldorado, Cadillacs, or trucks. Worked on a line that built a new engine every thirty seconds, or so it seemed. My job was hookup, which meant I put pistons into cylinders. Sounds simple, but it really wasn't. The rings had to be in the right place when you rammed the piston home, as they said. Eventually got it. Had to. Twenty-minute breaks, and that started when the line shut down. When the bell rang, you had to be on the job or else. "Else" meant the line just took off without you. Of course, there were relief men who would help if you got into trouble. That is, if they weren't hobnobbing with the boss or union rep or maybe a girlfriend. Didn't call them often; they would get upset. Second shift had some really different people. People who started their day at about noon or 1:00 p.m. They stayed up late, and whether they were watching TV or partying, they never went to bed before 2:00 a.m. Most of the people were good people who were trying to make a living. Most everybody there loved their cars. I really didn't like second shift or this job and just did the best I could until Coldwater Road called me back. This plant was much dirtier than Fisher Body, and even though I didn't work in the area where they made the cylinders or rods, when I left I had that smell. I started to feel like I was just a number—one of many brothers and sisters who would very soon feel the same way. January 7, 1985 is a date that will be remembered forever in the lives of many of the GM rank and file. It also was the day that I received notice that Fisher Body wanted me back. Hurray! I couldn't go back, though, unless I quit V-8. Well, I couldn't do that unless I was sure I wouldn't break seniority.

Illustration by Shannon Palmer

Department Eight—
Coldwater Road 1978

Get assigned job on tough line, have to learn to work pedal and move parts that look like hockey sticks through a two-stage press. Most of the jobs require tongs or the ability to put part in press and hit two buttons. Press comes down and makes cutout. My job about four stages down requires me to take the part off a conveyor and put it in a press and then push down on the pedal then move the part to another station within the same press and make another cut on the part by pressing on the pedal. This is all done in the same die. Well, in the beginning the parts came, and I was able to do it one at a time. Then the line started to move faster, and I wasn't able to keep up. Parts went on the floor, and my job was to catch up after the line quit for break. Eventually I caught on to it, but it took a long time. These parts were called drip-edge moldings; they went onto Buicks and Cadillacs—big cars. I used to wear rubber gloves that would tear after an hour or two. I would carry three pairs of gloves to every job. My hands were raw at the end of the day. I worked with some outstanding people who would work you very hard but would also help and even take your job for a while if need be. We all had a goal, and that was to do the best and get done early. You see, we had a standard* to make, and once we got it we could relax and play cards. I really enjoyed the people in department eight. They were a mix of older and younger employees, and all had the same goal—produce and be rewarded by a break at the end of the day.

Transfer to Department Nine

Finally learned the job and decided to go for a better job. Department nine was the area where they built seatbelts for every car and truck in GM. Remember when you would see the Fisher Body logo on the seatbelts on all of the GM vehicles? They came from the Fisher Body Coldwater plant. There were ladies who sewed, and there were people who made the seatbelts, from the station where they cut the right length for the belt to the line to the area where they were put in the plastic covers. I landed a job in the area where they put the covers on the belts, and I loved it. Of course, my hands had to get used to the different job, and therefore were raw again for a while. I worked with several guys in this area. The ladies seemed to work where they could handle the parts more closely and on the sewing line. We worked upstairs in the plant. It used to get very hot, and with very few fans, you just started sweating, and so you worked very hard in the morning in hopes that you were almost finished by just after lunch. There were four of us who would put the seatbelts in the plastic sleeves. Being new, I couldn't go as quickly as the regulars, and therefore I was behind. The three guys would chip in for me about an hour after lunch, and I would be done within a half hour. They didn't have to, but they just wanted to. They saw that I was trying to do the best that I could.

Within a couple of weeks, and after a little training by the older worker, I learned to do it better. I no longer needed them to help me reach production goals. I was part of the group. It was a great group. There was one old setup man whom I really got to know well. His name escapes me, but he was there every day about one hour early and had everything setup for the worker. He was a short man of about fifty or so who loved his coffee in the morning. I never even drank coffee until I got in the shop. In the afternoon, he would always have a couple of seven-and-sevens. He had a toolbox and a separate area where he would be if anybody needed anything. He used to smoke cigars, too. He said, "If you're going to make it here, you have to have something to look forward to after the work is done." I loved baseball, and the union had a softball team. I joined the team. Met lots of people and had lots of fun. Now it's late spring 1979, and GM decides that they have too many workers or parts or something; I didn't really know and didn't care. Got six weeks off with 95 percent pay during the summer. This was the beginning of the layoffs. Coldwater Road had a plan that they would rotate within the group. Six weeks off, then back to work, and the next person in line would take six weeks off. This worked for a while. Eventually it caught up with all of us, and the hatchet came down.

Permanent Layoff—October 1981

Prior to this I had met my Amy, who became my wife in March of 1980. We had been married just over a year when the brakes set in. I mean no money and no job. Wait for unemployment check in the mail and then apply for subpay. She had also been working at a plant in Corunna that had run into some hard times. She got laid off too, only she had no subpay. I never expected to be off more than a couple of months, but when it turned into three, four, etc, I started to wonder whether I would have a job. In April of 1982, I was running out of subcredits. They were supposed to last a year, but after four months, they started to take two credits per week and then five per week. I didn't want to run out, so I applied for a job at a dealership in Owosso—a Ford dealership at that! Herb Stoner Ford. Found out I could sell cars and liked it. I was twenty-five years old, and I became the number one salesman at the dealership within two months. Won trips, bonuses etc. Saved up enough money, took a gamble and bought a house with the $7000 we had in the bank. It was a cool home. Only had a couple hundred bucks left, but knew I could make more. Bought the home on a land contract for $32,000. Three bedrooms, two baths, two-car garage. Nice area in Owosso's northeast side, across from the school. By the end of summer, I had forgotten about GM. I was selling cars at a rate of about one every other day. Averaged seventeen per month during the worst time in the car industry. 1982 had interest rates of over 14.5 percent at the bank and close to 18 percent on car loans at times. President Ronald Reagan said a new beginning needed to happen, but when would it? He had been saddled with trouble with the Iran hostage crisis, which he took care of, but gas prices were at record levels. That will sound familiar later. Continued to sell cars in 1983, but all of a sudden the shop decides to call me back. Wow! What do I do? I loved selling cars, but had no insurance though I had a wife and little baby girl. Asked my father-in-law what I should do. Asked my wife. After many moments of discussion, I decided that I needed to talk to my boss and tell him that I either needed to become the manager of the store or I was going back to the shop. Herb Stoner was a cool owner; he had a unique personality. He loved a winner, but said that I was too young to be the boss and that the rest of the salespeople wouldn't respect me or listen to me. He just couldn't make me the general boss. I left! It's funny how people influence your decisions and affect your life, and Herb Stoner affected mine. I respect him for that. Sometimes you don't realize that you are having an effect on somebody, but you do. I'd like to think that I have had some influence on the people I've come in contact with.

June 1983
Back to GM Coldwater Road

Nice to be back! Not! The place hadn't changed except that the management had gotten more aggravating. I mean they weren't happy. I could see that they had become increasingly more antagonistic. Of course, I wasn't used to working this hard, and it felt like I was a new hire—again! Several of the jobs had now been changed, and the production had been increased without any improvement in the job. Typical GM. It is an engineering move and time to restudy the job with the same people who had been doing it for years. 20 percent increase in production. The people who were running that job leave the job because they called those of us with less seniority back. We can't achieve the production numbers, and so the boss is upset and under pressure from his boss. It is not the same as it was when I left in 1981. The auto industry is in a state of change. Fisher Body is under stress to cut costs or lose work for GM. I thought they were owned by GM. Well, we were a parts supplier. Our plant could have gone into plastics but didn't. Fools! They lost lots of potential work that other suppliers got as GM started to go into plastics. They eventually didn't need the parts we produced, and I would be laid off again in October 1984. This time I get picked up by the V-8 plant from the newly formed jobs bank. I worked at V-8 for just three months. It was a dirty plant. Tough union rank-and-file caucus. They would come out to the floor and take care of their special people and that was it. I worked on second shift on the hookup V-8 line. Three days or you were gone. It was interesting and tough. A sixteen-minute break and the line would start running whether you were there or not. Bathrooms were a long way from the line, so after you did your business it would be time to get back to work. Couldn't get ahead like at Coldwater Road in years past. I wondered what had I done. *Who is running this ship?* Coldwater Road calls me back in January 1985, and I'm happy to go back. My friend Dan Scollon decides not to go back. He is going to be a foreman at V-8. He was from Coldwater Road too. I'm tired of getting laid off. He does get his supervisor job, and I go back to Coldwater Road. I, too, was in line to get a promotion, but couldn't see myself on second shift for life. Choices! Work another year at Coldwater Road. Same type of work, only a little bit harder. Employees aren't as happy as when I started, but still come to work every day. Another layoff occurs in May 1986. *Who's running this place?* Stay out on layoff, because it is going to be summer soon and I don't want to be picked up by the Chevy truck plant, which was hiring. Finally sign up for the jobs bank because I hear that Auduburn, or GMSPO as it is called today, is hiring. Before I even get home from signing up, I have received a call to report to Flint Metal Fab for a physical. What! My wife tells me when I get home. I freak. It is on Bristol Road. Never been there and don't know anybody from there. Walk in and take physical and they want me to start that night, kind of like when I started at GM. I decline. I start the next Monday. After all, it was summer, and I was going to be a welder. Flint Metal Fab had landed a new job that required at least 350 welders on the C-cradle line. Flint Metal Fab was a hard-working, hot-welding, and stinky sheet metal plant that is a unit of the Local 659—home of the Sit-downers. Learned what it was to make a buck and also how hard some of the employees worked to earn a buck for this company. Not many women in this facility. Lots of heavy work. Very noisy plant. Ear plugs in all day, that's for sure. Welders had a certain toughness about them. They didn't take any crap, and they didn't like anybody who couldn't carry his own weight, and they let you know it one way or another. They had production, and they wanted to get done before it got too hot in the afternoon. We got it done. Our quality was also very good. Metal Fab had very good teachers of the trade. I worked in the C-cradle area. We used to have meetings with our boss, and he would tell us how well we were doing. In fact, we would find out how much money we made for the company in any given month. Sometimes it was as much as $50,000. Problem with that is the bean counters decided that only the assembly plants needed to make money. They made us cut our prices to move us toward breaking even. Remember, this was only one cradle. The W-cradle area made money on every cradle. This was 1987. Ten years with the company. Three different plants, and also now have this additional seniority date of 1-7-85. Still had recall rights to Coldwater Road. Flint Metal Fab had hired off the street in July 1985, and they would hire new employees. Little did they know that they would always be low-seniority employees. Most of the employees hired were related union officials' kids or salary kids—about two hundred of them. Didn't realize it then, but they probably protected my job because they were related and because of the politics of getting new work and such. Read on. Our plant soared from 1987 to 1990. The Berlin wall had fallen, and freedom was coming to the eastern block, which had been controlled by the Soviet Union forever, it seemed. George Bush got elected by saying "No new taxes!" He really got elected on the coattails of Reagan, who was loved even by the rank and file, even though the union wanted us to vote democratic. Desert Storm! Everybody remembers that. A tremendous success story. No casualties. The country was doing well. And so was I. I had money. There was overtime and stability for a change in a plant that had it going. The plant landed another new job—the GM10 it was called. It was a part that would go under all the new midsize cars. Also, we landed the sheet metal for the new, small Chevy S10. Clinton gets elected without a majority of popular vote. Ross Perot takes 13 percent of vote from Bush. Economy rolls! Public loves truck and becomes increasingly dependent on foreign oil. Life is good. Gas is still cheap at $1.299 per gallon. Stock market jumps and goes crazy because of all the high technology and the markets overseas in Europe. Japan continues to make inroads in the quality of small cars. Consumers Reports say they're best in quality. In 1993, our plant continues to hire area hires. Most have more seniority than me with the 1-7-85 area hire date. They get better jobs as soon as they walk in the door. People are bitter. They form groups that are quite diverse to take on the union. The black caucus wants to support us, but some area hires are undecided. Local 659 is an amalgamated union with several plants they represent. Our officials are out of sync with the membership. Workers Form a group called Your Original Union (YOU). Members are from Metal Fab, V-8, GMSPO, and Chevy downtown. Prepare for over eight weeks, including a confrontation with the leadership at the meeting hall. Several hundred people are there. I get to the microphone to be recognized by the president, Joe Duplanty, and a member of the caucus motions for the question. I had them on the ropes and they wouldn't let me speak. That was March 1993.

Flint Metal Fabricating Plant, Bristol Rd. Flint, MI (As it is today)

GMSPO (Auduburn) Plant Swartz Creek, MI (As it is today)

January 14, 1985

Finally get word that quitting V-8 isn't quitting GM, just quitting V-8. What! Anyway, as it turns out, I'm not alone as GM starts to gear up for spring of 1985. In the meantime, the date of 1-7-85 has been put into our contract; what it all means, nobody knows. The union said they negotiated this date to protect the higher-seniority employees. GM hires off the street in 1985. Of course this was only at selective plants, and of course the new hires were union staff kids and salary staff kids only. They might have also had to hire some minorities, including women, to fulfill the affirmative action requirement. Coldwater Road brings a lot of their laid-off employees back, at least all the 1977 seniority employees. Work is steady for about a year. Never get too comfortable. Nice to see some of my old friends, such as Scott Griffin, Danny Martin, Mike Cicallo, Terry Gutteriz, and Tony Vargo. Winter came and GM again had overproduced. Things began to slow down. Started to get involved in the Old News Boys campaign. Not too much, as they would only allow so many employees off the job, and with my seniority I didn't have much chance of working a corner. Started hearing rumors about another layoff in the works. The company went temp for six weeks with high seniority getting it first. That carried through to about May. All of a sudden, the company decided to go permanent, and I was axed again. Didn't expect it, but I should have. I'm off, but can put in to go to work at another plant anytime in the jobs bank. Hear the truck plant is hiring, but don't want to work there. After all, I'm getting 95 percent of my pay and it is getting to be summer. Hear that the parts plant in Swartz Creek is hiring, so I elect to put in for placement. Nope, I get the call and letter from Flint Metal Fabricating. What's this? Luck of the draw? I've got to report for physical immediately. They want me to start the same day. I elect to start on Monday so as not to screw up my paychecks. Walk into the plant and find out that this plant is huge. Full of presses and people everywhere. They take me back to the frame area, where the welding is done. I'm going to be a welding technician. Of course, I've never done this before. Get a little training, get the gear on, and practice for a day. On the next day, I am allowed to practice for a few hours, and then I get sent to the line with a trainer. Don't do too badly on the line of the final assembly C-cradle. Trainer says, "Report to this station at 6:00 a.m." Meet the boss; boss asks, "How do you feel?" I say I'm nervous. Guys on line call me rookie, but most are willing to work with me. Fellow workers more willing to help me get better than at V-8 plant. Part of the reason, I figure, is that there is a production goal that is attainable. Everybody needs goals—realistic ones, I might add. I once got into a heated discussion offsite with the plant manager about goals that are attainable. He was focused only on the big picture. Typical. He never put a helmet on in 110-degree heat while burning metal, making perfect welds every time on 720 frames per day, wearing all this protective gear, and going nonstop for two and a half hours till break. He was drinking coffee and reading last night's report on the press line. I still feel that Flint Metal Fab had the toughest group of individuals ever seen—hard-working bastards who didn't mind getting into it with management, especially when they were right.

Black, white, or Hispanic, when you strap that helmet on, you are just one of the welders, sweating all the way down to the skin. I used to lose 5 lbs. a day in the summer. I began to settle into my job at Metal Fab. We got a new contract in 1987—one of the best. Chairman Jack Brown was very tough, but charismatic. He was one of the few chairmen not to have an ego. At least not to me. If he came down on the floor, the foreman ran and hid. There were two foremen who did not, and I eventually worked for both of them. One was Sam Cross and the other was Larry Polzin. They loved confrontation. They didn't always win, but they kept you on your toes. Anyway, this contract we won allowed the members the right to an open-door policy, which meant that if and when you met the production goal, you were able to do something else. You didn't have to clock out. Most of us on the line left when we were done with our production—100 percent, no less. The plant was extremely profitable; it made $45,000 per month according to the records. The frame plant held up the rest of the plant. However, some of the employees got into trouble on the outside, and by the next contract we were told that we had to change. We didn't have to clock out, but we had to stay in the plant. Most of us tried to sneak out and were successful. If you got caught, you would be penalized. Well, things are starting to get tougher for the union as global competition is starting to take hold. We really don't believe it, though. The S-10 is selling, and so are the trucks. GM has pretty much given up on the small car except for Saturn. Jack Brown left and went into the International Union, and so did Jim Stevens, another chairman of Metal Fab who was good. In the meantime, GM is still hiring periodically from plants that are downsizing, and Metal Fab is still picking them up. We are getting employees from Saginaw and other Flint plants, Lansing facilities, and even plants as far as Detroit and Pontiac. All the new hires are coming in with 1/7/85 seniority with their OGM date attached to it, which means that most of the employees were older employees with 1969, 1970, 1971, or 1972 hire dates from their previous plants. So, if they have 1/7/85 seniority and I have 1/7/85 seniority, then we go to hire-in date from the beginning. Most of them received better jobs than me even though I worked at Metal Fab since 1986. Hell, this is 1992 or early 1993. RESENTMENT! The new work we got was from the sweat off my brow, not theirs, yet they're getting the better opportunities and jobs. No way! I started a fight for our rights to no avail. Ran against the caucus and found out what politics was all about. Actually thought I would win. Why run for office if you're not thinking you can improve the situation? Met lots of people, and I wouldn't trade the experience for anything. Learned a lot about people. Found out that the people I thought were my friends really weren't. Found out that some people really have trouble with color. Found out that it's all about what you can do for me. I live in such a little world. Votes are won by a couple of drinks or a retiree dinner before the election. I ran for office because I thought that the 1/7/85 date was a farse and needed to be corrected. Gypsies, that's all we were. We moved from plant to plant with no loyalty, just a number. I remember feeling this way in late 1984 at V-8. It is now spring of 1993. I form a group called Your Original Union—what the union used to be. Dan Scollon runs with me. An old-time friend from Coldwater Road who is now working at V-8, Danny Martin, was also going to run with us, but he chickened out. We had been called "the three amigos" by the caucus before the election campaign got started. I eventually got lots of support and built a platform and a complete ticket.

1987—GM Metal Fab

Just got transferred to the C-Cradle cross-member area. Here is a tough area!
Very demanding. In fact, the boss says that I won't like it here. His name is
Polzon—Larry Polzon. He is a former hourly worker who turned foreman.
He knew all the tricks, so they said. I actually got along with him very
well. He drew a line in the sand, and if you crossed it, you knew where you
stood—penalty. He had a great crew working for him: Mike Cicalo, Scott
Griffin, and Duane Vieau, to name a few. There was also Rod and Jimmy.
We were all good welders. Even little Joe and his partner were good welders.
He decided to go on the warpath. He penalized everybody. If you were a
quarter inch off on your weld, then you would get penalized. He looked at
every part. You never knew when it was your turn. In addition, there had been
some discrepancies over how many parts had been built during the previous
day. He blamed all of us. We all knew who it was, but we wouldn't tell. In
fact, none of us would even let the boss know we knew. One of the groups
had been jacking parts on their counter. You see, we used to get done with
our production and be able to leave the plant without clocking out. We were
falling a hundred parts short of production, or a day behind. It didn't take
long to figure out who was doing it, but the company never did anything

about it. Instead, they just made us work overtime. Larry instead penalized these employees for missing welds or weld skips. Larry was one of the best foremen I ever worked for. If it was happening here, in the C-Cradle, one of the most profitable cradles in the plant, then I believe that it was happening all over. After a conversation with a long-time Buick employee, I learned that I was right. It's not that the people didn't want to work; it was that they had learned the ropes and had also learned that the boss needed his number. Today, those numbers are calculated on a computer and there is no discrepancy. You can always conflict over downtime. Downtime! That was one of my favorite things to challenge the boss about. The union eventually gave up the issue because it was considered noncompetitive. I remember one day on which I had written "downtime" for the GM10 final assembly. I had it figured as one amount for the final amount, and the boss had another. The boss took my clipboard and threw it off the back wall—a cement wall at that. He was furious. I was the negotiator for the whole group. I held my ground. All ten of the rest of the group stood with me, and I won that day. Get it? I won that day, but not the next week. The boss kept an eye on me during the rest of the week. I'm sure everyone can relate to that. Regardless, those three years were the best for GM and the rest of the corporation. There were incentives and bonuses for all of us. Greed! Can we do it for less cost and more profit? What! You're already making $45,000 per month just on the C-cradle. I sat in on the meetings. They blamed the people—the guys who were working on the outside during company time. Hey, I don't blame them about that. I also don't blame the guys trying to make more cash. We were all hungry then. When I say hungry, I mean we had ambition. The guys who were doing that kind of work should have been offered a job on salary somewhere. After all, the foremen usually worked at least ten to twelve hours per day and for more pay. Instead, penalize them! And they did! In fact, the employees almost lost their jobs. Another opportunity lost. Hey, these guys were ambitious. I was too, but not to that extent. 1990 saw no more clocking out, but also no more leaving when we were done. The union just couldn't get it together. They were constantly fighting the fact that many workers were still leaving the plant and they couldn't control it. Eventually the whole thing had to end because they had no recourse and the public wouldn't stand for it. This was too bad; it was a good thing, actually. It gave the average worker an opportunity to succeed. That's huge in the eyes of the average person. Maybe I'm not such a loser. We all know that there are people who drink after lunch in every profession, and it is no different than working at Motorola or Nextel. The only difference is that the employees aren't wearing welding gear, but sport coats. If you think I'm kidding, just ask your neighbor. That's not a yes or a no regarding the opportunity to communicate with the people who make your company work in a relaxed atmosphere. The big thing is to remember to get it right the first time. That's what people remember. Just hope they remember you!

Why Old Plants Are Bulldozed!

Have they served their useful life, or is there another reason? I think that there might be an underlying reason somewhere. After all, the shops were filled with chemicals that we all know will kill. When I was hired on in 1977, I didn't know any of this. Not that it would have stopped me from making more money than I ever did. I saw many people who lost fingers and maybe more, but that was the nature of the business. The biggest issue had to be the chemicals, whether they were the ones in the air or the ones we handled that went into the presses or the chemicals that were used to clean up the messes that were created. Any time you deal with chemicals, you might get a reaction. The wrong stuff put with the right stuff, and you get the idea—a mess. Kind of like 9-11. It's really not anybody's particular fault; it just happens. Who pays? The company that provided you with the opportunity to make a good living, or the government that allowed this type of stuff to go on? Coldwater Road had many types of chemicals, including asbestos, lead, die-castmetal, and chrome plating. Even headliners were dangerous. Headliners were made of fiberglass and caused lots of problems for many a worker, yet they continued to work there. President Michael Bennett of Local 326 finally did something about the Coldwater Road situation with chrome plating and the lead and the die-casting area. Instead of fixing the problem, the company did away with the jobs, and then the loss of good jobs started to disappear. This was 1983. President Mike Bennett had good intentions, but it resulted in the loss of jobs. He also made a name for himself that he would carry with him to the new Saturn plant, where he became president again. Nice! I remember working in both areas. The situation could have been corrected. Back then, if there was any problem with the system, the company was all too eager to remove and outsource the work. After all, we were dealing with the Fisher Body management—probably the worst group I ever worked for. They were assholes, considering the fact that they had the opportunity to go into plastics before anybody else but were too greedy making money at what they were doing to pursue plastics. Plastics were cheaper and produced less scrap than metal. In fact, GM encouraged them to develop something in plastics. There was no investment and lack of vision. Needless to say, we lost jobs, and then I went to V-8. I didn't even work in the place where they made the rods, but every day that I came home from there I had the smell of chemicals on me. There was so much going on at V-8 that most people didn't know what they were stepping in or what they were working with. In case you haven't been following this little escapade that GM has been engaged in, let me tell you that both Coldwater Road and the old V-8 plant have been torn down and had cement poured over them. Reminds me of Chernobol, Russia. Where was the U.S. government? Politics! Build a new plant and get a new tax break. In fact, just claim that you're going to put some new equipment in a plant and you get the government of Michigan to show up. I tell you, that this is what the workers of Michigan are all about. They should be proud of hanging on to their jobs and producing such high quality products. Please! Every top union official is there patting you on the back, but they don't know the whole picture, nor do they care. We are saving our jobs for today, but who will save them tomorrow? With fewer and fewer union workers, the trend is to continue to downsize. China is the new America. Why? They don't care about their environment. Some day they will, though. GREED! Is Toyota doing more for their workers than GM? No! The phrase is not "what I can do for you?" but "how much can you do for me in less time?" Jobs used to be bid by volume and cost, but now they're bid by cost per part, per hour, and how little they must pay the worker. The worker is the one who wants to buy the product. Wake up, GM and Ford! (I can't say Chrysler because they have been bought by the Germans.) The last generation of workers is getting older, and if you don't decide to hire new American workers, then who will buy your product when they're gone? After all, retirees can't afford them. "Legacy costs," the upper management says. Wrong. They're the loyal ones still buying GM, Ford, etc. What needs to happen is to finally get a politician who has been through tough times, not a career politician like we have in Mr. Carl Levin. Not that he hasn't done good things for the state, but his time is up. Dave Camp is another career politician who hasn't ever been really challenged, and yet he was the one to cast the final "yes" vote on CAFTA. I'm sick about it. He has cost us more jobs than he has ever created. When you campaign with the idea that you're a so-called good old boy who takes care of certain people, and you advertise this, then we all know that you have no message and no leadership. He's been in seven terms and really hasn't thought of anything that is relevant except for the big vote for CAFTA and Bush. This didn't stop any of the A.O. Smith jobs from leaving the state right under his nose. Sign of the times? Find a new job in the unemployment line. I had to. Why are old plants bulldozed? Because the politicians can't see past the green bucks of re-election. Anyway, both plants that I worked at are no longer; they're just a pile of cement, except that there might be a plaque mentioning that at one time there were thousands of Americans who worked for their livings and paid taxes and raised families near there, but it is all gone now. Henry Ford might be done, but he at least respected his workers. Back in his day, five bucks a day was great, and they bought his product because of it. Hey, he still made millions off of it. Lee Iacocca had vision; don't let Toyota steal the American dream. After all, we aren't all made to go to a four-year accredited college and give the university $50,000 plus for an average education that, had I worked at a credible company, might have enabled me to be promoted from within, and I would have learned the ropes on the line like it used to be. Experience! It will come back to haunt them. The new leadership has no experience on the shop floor. The last of the bosses to come off the floor did so in 1985. That's sad. Seems like things started to go down hill after that. Gypsies, Greed, and Politics. Get the picture.

5-93

I have the perfect ticket. I have employees from every plant in officer positions. The only problem is that I want to run for president, but after discussion, I agree to run for first VP

I can't remember some of my favorite people, but the "Cookie Man" was one of the best. He was an older black man who wanted change at V-8. He called

31

me at 3:00 a.m. on the morning of Election Day and said he couldn't keep his eyes open anymore and asked if someone would come to relieve him. After all, he wasn't even running, and the ballot boxes he was watching could get tampered with. I had just gone to bed at 1:00 a.m., and I couldn't respond, as I had been up campaigning since 5:00 a.m. the previous morning. I had two beautiful kids and hadn't seen them in weeks. My wife supported me the whole way; she is an inspiration to me and the best mom you could ever ask for. She rarely asks for anything except my time. I love her. Election Day comes and I'm all over, especially the union hall of Local 659. Remember the dinner? Retirees come out and vote for the incumbents. international reps were everywhere. Even Jack Brown, former president of Local 659, was there. He remembers me and kind of basically goes through the motions. Results: All incumbents win. Reality sets in. I just spent $1000 of my own money and a few days of my vacation, plus three or four weeks away from my family, to try to make a difference. I was called a loser by many. But really, all that effort meant that people weren't ready to change. Change is something that must evolve, I guess. A new product line called UW frame is coming in soon; however, employees must work by the hour or in stages. There are fewer people again from GM-10. There are seven per station, but some of the work is more difficult. There is no incentive. Most of the plant is running overtime. The sheet metal areas are all working, but they don't produce enough quality stuff, that's why they are on OT. This has been going on for years, but because of the frame area that made so much money for the plant, no one noticed. As the old frames start dying, no new work replaces it. Sheet metal doesn't get any better, and therefore the plant suffers. It needs more output. We get new dies in a 1996 agreement—GMT— 800 work for fenders and hoods. These are the dies that will get taken out during the strike of 1998. Along with the new work come new sacrifices. Hit the frames. Can't get done early anymore. Employees start to try moving out with transfers. Applications for different jobs. Company puts freeze on employees who are welders leaving the group. Why? They don't want to train new people for these jobs, and the production will suffer. Meanwhile, the union agreed to changes in the way the work is handled, including not getting done early. People want out rather than work on the line with no incentive. More employees hired again from the area hire as 1/7/85 OGM of 1976, or earlier. New employees go into open group. Of course, they have more time than the majority of the welders. Guess what? Keep welding. You don't have enough seniority to get out of welding. Why? Nobody wants to be a welder now that there is no incentive and they just hired a bunch of area hires who have more OGM than you and walked in with 1/7/85 seniority. You get the picture. Management won't let the highly trained workers out of welding because of the cost to train and the fact that production has increased. The same union people win again. They must be doing something right. Of all the hypocrisy is the fact that GM hired two hundred people in 1995 who will never build any seniority because of the 1/7/85 seniority date. In fact, GM hired one hundred or so employees in Metal Fab during May or June of 1985, and they haven't gained a day of seniority. When you think about it, everything evolves around longevity. It is the reason you stay with a company. Benefits are supposed to get better, as are vacation time and job opportunities, but in the case of GM, because of the 1/7/85 date, employees were being stripped of their chance to have better jobs. The better you did, the more they wanted. At any time, they would call for emergency measures and say you must work OT or Saturdays. It is all about the money. There is no structure and no accountability by management. Management used to be hired off the floor, but now only college grads were considered. They don't have a clue. I've now moved on. I decided to go on third shift to avoid the white shirts. It is 1996. My friends also went on third shift. We are still building quality products, but it seems like we're going nowhere. I now have spent twenty years with this company. Seems like I was hired on yesterday. A lot has changed, and yet a lot has remained the same. I miss the innocence of being twenty years old and being very thankful for my job. I miss the smiles on people's faces when they came into work. After all, we were all twenty, or maybe eighteen or nineteen, when we hired in. I really didn't think about the health benefits or retirement package we were getting. I was having fun and working hard with a lot of other young people who were also having fun. Third shift was now for the hermits or people who didn't have kids at home. Forget about the fact that you get 10 percent more; my kids were still growing up. In fact, I had a new one on the way. Eventually, the shift caught up with me. Of course. I had started a business and my wife wanted me home. I was missing out on stuff with my kids. Life is too short. During the time from 1997 to 2003, most everything at the shop was a blur. I had started my own real estate company and was focused on that. My wife and I also built a home in Owosso. Made a good living at GM, but didn't see how fast things were happening except for 1998, because of the strike of 1998.

1994

Working in the GM10 area on another Friday that was much the same as the last, I found myself getting anxious with my co-workers. I had been working with the same group for over two years. It seemed that every day brought a different challenge, whether it was with the boss over downtime or the lack of parts from the robot or the fact that my welding gun had been left in repair when I came in to work. Of course, all this was typical GM. But it's Friday, and that means the end of the week. I had been waiting on parts all morning, and it was only 10:00 a.m. I decided to sit down on a bench and let the parts build up. The other two co-workers did the same. The group in front of us also did the same after they had built their five full frames and sent out their rack. The boss came over and asked what I was doing, and I said I was waiting for parts. That was not exactly true, as the parts were coming; they were just not coming fast enough. I constantly had to bend over and pick up the parts from the conveyor, and I decided that I would wait until the co-worker had built up a little bank. This went on for the bulk of the hour. 11:00 a.m. was lunch time. Normally we would be almost done at this time, but today we had nearly double the amount needed to be done. After lunch, everybody wants to get done, but the robot hadn't been running at the right speed, so the parts were still coming slowly. I decided to go over and stand near the other employee and wait for the parts to be welded. As I stood there, I said things like "anytime," "come on," "let's go," and other antagonizing comments. Finally, the guy running the table, whom I was waiting for, puts down his helmet, and in one motion, grabs me with one hand, and with the other grabs me in the crotch, and lifts me up above his head. This worker was 6' 6" tall and weighed about 300 to 320 lbs. He was a very nice guy normally, but I had been heckling him, and he'd had enough. We called him Big Ron. Ron had a very quiet personality, carried himself well, and was not at all mean. I apparently pushed his button. He raised me up above his shoulders like I was one of the hogs or other animals that he raised on his farm. He walked over to a scrap gondola and asked the guys whether he should put me in there. The rest of the guys roared and said, "Do it." Well, thank you very much, he didn't. He put me down on my hands, or head first. I dodged a bullet. He could've put me in the scrap gondola if he wanted, and I would've been hurt. I was very thankful, but at the same time, embarrassed. He went back to work, and I waited for him to finish working before I went up to him and apologized. I bought him a Coke and said, "I'll see you tomorrow." We had been co-workers for two years, and I really didn't know him until that day. We became good friends after that. I found out he lived in Chesaning. He had a wife and two kids. He was a great guy who would do anything for you. He used to get the shaft a lot of times and have to do some of the toughest jobs because the foremen would use his size and the fact that he didn't have enough seniority to get a better job (the reason being the 1-7-85 hire date he also got saddled with.) He rarely complained. We rarely complained about the 1-7-85 date. We figured that was the way all the plants were. We thought Ford and Chrysler also were like that. We even thought Saturn was like that, but oh, no! This was a mastermind plan of the union to keep the people of the home plant safe from being overtaken by the older workers from plants that might be closed. Even though these members of the union had paid union dues longer and for more locals, they were considered outcasts, though not in the way that they were considered new hires; they were entitled to their service time and also their vacation pay. The members who had 1-7-85 seniority with an OGM date had to fight to get their vacation time off. They were not given preferential treatment in anything form getting a better job to getting time off for their families. They got time off when the people from the plant with more than 1-7-85 seniority didn't want it. They also go the jobs left over after the members of the plant with more than 1-7-85 seniority were satisfied. In fact, that meant welding for a number of years longer than what might have been necessary under the plans at Ford or Chrysler. The jobs that the members of 1-7-85 with OGM got were, most of the time, more strenuous and less rewarding. The membership suffered because of it. Was it their fault that their plant closed? I doubt it. The big reason behind the 1-7-85 date was to protect the locals from being overrun. They just wanted to have the same opportunity as when they hired in.

federal benefit is received for the same period of time that a UAW strike benefit was paid, repayment to the strike fund must immediately be made to continue eligibility for future strike insurance benefits.

2. Those members who are denied unemployment compensation because of the strike shall be paid benefits in the form of a loan which must be repaid to the strike fund immediately upon receipt of unemployment compensation. Failure to do so may result in legal action being taken. In order for members to receive a loan, they must continue to sign up weekly for unemployment compensation and file any appeals required by the state.

3. If a member receives a loan during the strike, which is later repaid during the strike, and the member subsequently exhausts his/her unemployment compensation during the strike, he/she will once again be eligible for benefits as long as the strike continues. If a member has failed to fully repay the loan, he/she will automatically be disqualified from any future benefits during the strike.

Strike Assistance will be paid in accordance with Administrative Letter dated August 1, 1994, Volume 44, Letter No. 2.

Roy O. Wyse
Secretary-Treasurer
International Union, UAW

SUMMARY OF UAW STRIKE ASSISTANCE RULES

Strike assistance shall be based on right in accordance with the rules and regulations approved by the International Executive Board.

The Strike Assistance Program shall be administered by the International Union UAW Strike Insurance Department in cooperation with the Local Union.

ELIGIBILITY RULES:

1. Only members of the Local Union on strike who were on the ACTIVE PAYROLL at the time the strike began shall be entitled to strike assistance.

2. You must participate in the strike activity assigned to you by the Local Union on the date(s) and time(s) specified. Participation in the strike shall include services on the Community Services Committee, picket line duty, strike information classes, strike kitchen duty, soliciting committee, lectures or other appropriate activities established by your Local Union.

3. A member must be in good standing the day before a strike commences to be entitled to strike assistance provided they meet the other qualifications.

4. A member who owes a reinstatement fee, back dues, a fine or a strike fund loan shall not be considered in good standing for the purpose of obtaining strike assistance.

5. Any member who is or becomes delinquent in his/her dues and later acquires good standing membership by paying his/her back dues and reinstatement fee at least one (1) year prior to a strike shall not be penalized for his/her delinquency.

6. Any member who is delinquent and does not pay his/her back dues and reinstatement fee at least one (1) year prior to a strike shall be penalized two (2) weeks strike benefits for his/her delinquency.

7. Probationary and new hires may become eligible for strike assistance only if they join the Union by paying the initiation fee and current month's dues prior to the strike taking place. In the event a worker has completed and signed an application for membership and a Union checkoff card has been forwarded to his/her Company prior to the strike taking place, he/she would be considered a member in good standing and would be entitled to strike assistance.

YOU ARE NOT ENTITLED TO STRIKE ASSISTANCE:

1. If you are unemployed prior to the strike.
2. If you are drawing sick and accident benefits.
3. If you are drawing Workers Compensation benefits.
4. If you earn $150.00 gross pay or more per week during the strike.
5. Any member who has been receiving sick and accident benefits during the strike will be entitled to strike benefits once he/she has been released by his/her doctor as being able to return to work, and they meet the other qualifications.

SCHEDULE OF BENEFITS:

1. Strike assistance shall be available UPON APPLICATION to all members who register and participate in the strike activity assigned to them by their Local Union under the rules established by the International Union.

2. A member shall accumulate strike assistance credits beginning with the 8th day of the strike (For this purpose, Saturdays and Sundays shall be used when determining the eight days.) For each day's pay missed due to the strike, Monday through Friday, a member shall receive one day's strike benefits at the prorated daily amount.

3. Strike assistance shall be made available to the member beginning on the 15th day of the strike.

4. Weekly benefits are $150.00 regardless of status.

5. Striking members will receive $30.00 per day for each day that they are on strike beginning with the 8th day of the strike Monday through Friday.

6. Members must pick up their benefit check on the day assigned to them by their Local Union or lose that week's benefit.

7. Any member who is eligible for strike benefits immediately preceding the termination of the strike will be paid an additional one (1) week's strike benefits.

BONUSES:

A. Any member who is drawing strike benefits during the week prior to the Thanksgiving Holiday will receive a bonus check equal to the regular strike benefits during that week.

B. Any member who is drawing strike benefits during the week prior to the Christmas Holiday will receive a bonus check equal to the regular strike benefits during that week.

INSURANCE BENEFIT

Upon approval by the International President and Secretary-Treasurer, the International Union, from its strike fund, will pay Group Life, Transition Bridge and Group Medical-Hospital Insurance Premiums, excluding dental, vision, audio and sick and accident premiums for striking members who participate in a strike activity assigned to them by the Local Union. These premiums will only be paid by the International Union after approval has been given by the International President and Secretary-Treasurer and then only after all contractual language and other obligations have been exhausted. Optional insurance coverage and rider policies will remain the responsibility of the member.

RULES REGARDING OTHER ASSISTANCE:

1. If it is determined, during the course of a strike, that you may be eligible for state or federal assistance, you must sign up for that benefit to maintain your eligibility in the Strike Assistance Program. If a state or

May 19, 1998—
Night Before the Strike of 1998

Third shift: Night starts out like any other night, except there is a feeling
something is going to happen soon; after all, the dies were gone and the union
had had their strike vote. We still hadn't heard anything from the union
officials about what the international Union had agreed to. We produced
out parts and finished about 5:30 a.m. No decision yet. "Report tomorrow"

is what the union said. I go home and find out when I wake up that Local 659 had walked out about 10:00 a.m. with Norwood Jewell, shop chairman, leading the charge. Norwood Jewell was a quiet type of guy, and a tough guy to figure out. He would be with you one day, and the next he would not be. Always did a good job in negotiating, though. He was a former foreman who turned union steward. Rose through the ranks. A deal cutter. Now he is waving a flag in front of the TV cameras. No deal this time! I call the union hall and find out what I'm supposed to do. They didn't call me. If I wanted to picket, I would have to sign up for duty. Picket duty! That is the only way you would receive any strike pay. It paid $150 dollars per week, or was it $100 per week? The international Union had control of the purse strings. You had to work your shift hours in four-hour blocks at least once a week. It was very exciting at first, with people screaming, horns blasting, and truckers stopping in front of the gates, blocking traffic. State troopers with there with lights flashing, getting out of their cars and trying to force the truckers to keep moving, but they just sat there. And when I say truckers, I mean semis—lots of them—maybe twenty or thirty of them in front of Flint Metal Fab. Talk about support! Not to mention the support of Krifan's Market, Donna's Donuts, and the many other restaurants that would be affected by the strike. There was always food and drink for the picketers, day and night. There were older retirees who would stop by. There hadn't been a strike since 1970, and before that, the big one of 1937. Well, Local 659 and Flint Metal Fab were reclaiming their roots. After a couple of weeks and no news of any progress, the membership wanted to know why. Well the reason was simple. We had worked for months stockpiling parts in warehouses and working overtime when none was needed. Our schedule wasn't that high. Cars and trucks weren't selling like they had been in 1977 or 1978, but we had been working like they were. It took a while, but with Local 651 joining us in the strike, the parts dried up and the plants at GM became idle. Actually, the plants at GM, such as the truck plant next door, were out after a day or so. The people wanted to know what was going on, but we on third shift didn't get any type of feedback. If you wanted to know, you had to go to the bar. Rumors were that GM had somehow planned to have the union walk out because they had overbuilt, and this was a way to know that their hopes of getting a 30+ market share were fading. After all, the execs had lots of stock options, and they didn't want the stock prices to fall. The biggest story was that our union vice president was seen at lunch with one of the top negotiators in Grand Blanc. They had been resting and enjoying a couple of cocktails together. It had been determined then, at that table, that the strike would be settled and the dies brought back to Flint in time. *In time* meant when a couple things had fallen in to place. One of those things was that the inventories were at comfortable levels, and another was that it was after the July 4 shutdown period. Don't get me wrong; I enjoyed every minute of the time off with my wife and kids. It did cost me about $10,000 in income based on the work schedule we were keeping. The funny thing for me was that I had just built a home and hadn't sold my other one. I burned through all my cash in those fifty-four days. I also started my own real estate company at the same time. Dummy! Every time I planned something at GM, I would be fooled. I thought that the company and union were on the same page in 1996, but things change fast in the auto industry. On day fifty-five, we are told to report back to work. It is a shock! The company calls for a meeting. They say they will strictly enforce the local agreement, but we were welcome back. We were not sure what that meant, but found out real soon. We were not to be late from break or lunch—not even by a couple minutes—or they would write us up. Eventually, the company had penalized enough people that they felt comfortable with negotiating a new agreement in 1999. We lose, but we also, because of the strike of '98, had secured some new future work. The union had agreed to some work rule changes and also to give up the welding jobs in the future for some new A-presses. What are A-presses? They were a new press capable of producing a lot more product in far less time making it a more efficient, more productive plant. That will get us more work, right? Well, more work meant more jobs, right? It used to be so. At this time it just meant maintaining the current employment. At least that is what the company said. After all, GM was going to invest some $30 million in our plant over the next three years. To GM, that is a drop in the bucket. They were making billions. It's nice that we get a little bit of their interest. Well, the $30 million finally showed up in the last year of the contract. In the meantime, our plant was losing work that was being replaced with new work that we didn't get allocated. Remember that word— *allocated*! Our plant no longer bid on work. The new work would be allocated based on performance, which meant if you didn't improve from last year, then you didn't get any new work. How convenient! If you had old equipment that would break down so much so that you didn't get the numbers, then I guess you didn't get considered for the new work. It was one plant against the other. This was something the union had fought in the past, but they now had no response. In the meantime, union-appointed people started charting our progress, hoping for improvement. Do you see something wrong with this picture? That's engineering. union-appointed people shouldn't do foreman or salary work. There was bickering among membership over who should do the charting with the clipboard. Remember, we're still welding, only we are very good at our job now, as we have over thirteen years of experience. We know how to make our job better. Every time we do, they want us to do another couple of parts per hour. They call it being productive, efficient, etc. It used to be that we had a number that we figured we could make a profit at, and that's what we did. Now they're trying to trim costs by raising production without merit pay or even a token suggestion of pay. "We are a team" was the cry! "Strap on a helmet if we are a team." We started going through plant managers, which I'd known for a long time is not good for a plant. After all, I've been through quite a few. It is 2002, and it is time for a change. We have a new plant manager with lots of charisma; his name is Scott Whybrew. He is a year younger than me. Wow! He has tremendous ideas and lots of drive. I transfer to first shift.

2002

It is much different on first shift than third shift. A lot more people. Didn't realize how much older the work force had gotten. I had been gone for almost six years. Most of the membership that was on first shift could retire, but they needed a push.

Back to our new plant manger, Scott. He had ambition that I hadn't seen since the late '70s. He walked the plant floor. But he walked the floor to meet his co-workers, not his employees. He had a happy smile, a great personality, and he was professional. On Fridays he even wore jeans. He would be on the floor for support and to listen to our concerns, and he would not forget them. Within days, things would get changed. Our plant started to improve, even with all the old equipment. Why? Positive thinking and positive leadership. We established new records on several old machines that couldn't have been attained without positive leadership and a skilled work force. The plant won recognition from the corporation. What about jobs? Well, that might come, but we needed new investment. A $60 million investment from GM was made. Big announcement! We would get two new presses and a new blanker. No more welding. GM was sending that to Pontiac, which was under another boss. It was sad, because we were the best,at welding for years. In fact, if you remember the Chevy Astro van, we built the frame for over twenty years. It still remains the standard of durability among vans, and it was a great people mover. Back to the announcement. All of the press was there. Also there were the international reps; Richard Shoemaker, plant manager; Scott Whybrew, regional director; Assistant Regional Director Duane Suckswertd; and the most important person was Governor Jennifer Granholm. They wanted to be part of something that they thought could never be done. Hey, it was always there, and it still is. Like I said earlier, Flint has some of the hardest-working people in the world. At least, I've come to think so. Anyway, it all comes down to willingness to bend and work together. One note is that the corporation has always tried to get one over on us, and that philosophy just won't work today. Scott Whybrew prepared a big meal for the whole membership, celebrating fifty years at our plant. I'd like to thank all the hard-working men and women of the rank and file for their talents in providing entertainment and preparing food. Scott Whybrew got promoted to another location soon after the celebration. Just prior to his leaving, I had the opportunity to go to an offsite at Baker College with him. It was a tremendous success. Everybody takes a little bit with them, and I'll tell you this: the man was questioned repeatedly about what GM was going to do with our plant, and he said that if we continued to improve, we would be there in the future for our children. Positive! There was only one thing that I couldn't get him on. I asked him in one of our sessions why he set such high goals that seemed unattainable. He said they were attainable. Please! Our plant had just raised our efficiency 30 percent in one year, and he expected us to do that again? "Figure it out," I said. If he had only expected 10–15 percent improvement for the next year, we might have had a chance. I told him that 30 percent plus 30 percent the next year is not 60 percent, it's like 70 percent plus, and I'm not an economist. The membership still respected him. He leaves and so does our asst. plant manager. Something big is going to happen. A new guy comes in with a whole different approach. Still, he is another nice guy, but make no mistake, he is here to do one of two things: either close the place or make it lean and mean. When people retire, he doesn't replace them. Temporary layoffs consolidate jobs, which gives us more of a team concept. We are the last plant to come on board with this concept. He eliminates job rights and seniority rights on choosing jobs. You rotate jobs on the hour, not even by the day. You fly dies and work on electrical keyboards normally run by trained people who have separate classifications. He cuts employment by 30 percent in the first six months. Nobody notices because they are on temporary layoff and will be back in a year. Only problem is that we're not getting any new jobs. New presses arrive. Our skilled trades put them in and do a great job. Find out that there are only going to be six jobs per shift total—a maximum of eighteen plus trades. However, they're going through transition, too. The area these presses are taking at one time had five or six times the number of employees, not counting inspectors, additional truck drivers, etc. You get the picture. I watched them put these presses in. I saw all the concrete poured. It was sometimes eighteen inches or two feet thick. We had lots of dies, but no workers. These new presses were also engineered to change sets of dies in less than a few minutes. Incredible! My question is, why only two presses in a facility with everything going for it? The plant has high ceilings; is close to the airport, I-75, and I-69; and it has an experienced workforce. Oh yeah, during the '98 strike, it was said by upper management that they wanted to get Flint Metal Center down to 1,200 employees or less so it would be easier to control.

What GM forgets is that these people love the cars and trucks that they build. They see the quality. They talk to their friends. They have their families buy the vehicles they build. We love our product. Take away our pay and benefits, and you take away the heart and soul of your corporation—the bigger and better. You can't be a bean counter if there are no beans to count. Finally, we were out of welding. It is dying in our plant. Not much left. There was only Aluminum, which I was trained in but never really enjoyed. I became a fork truck driver. I loved it. It really was challenging in the beginning. I got a fresh start. Learned every job in the plant that they would let me do. Lots of older workers on these jobs—the last of the real, established jobs. The new plant manager still wanted to cut this work force. Too many drivers—the life blood of the factory—the product movers. He felt they could do more. He installed screens with logins for the drivers. He wanted to know what they were doing every moment. He eliminated jobs. He also shut down lines in the process. He didn't care. No job was secure. He consolidated supervisor jobs, demoted some, retired some, and really destroyed everything that Scott Whybrew had built in regard to trust. It was typical of GM. Some things in a business need to remain constant, and one is the positive influence of a leader, whether it is someone like Lee Iacocca or someone like Scott Whybrew. When your life is counting on someone to lead and all that person does is think about himself, you're trapped, and if you are able to get out of the trap, then you go for it. It was 2006. Lots of work was gone at Metal Fab now, and more people were doing nothing. GM announces that 30,000 jobs will be eliminated. Buyouts are coming. There are early outs, but you must have thirty years by the end of 2006 to qualify. Early outs provided $35,000 cash and full retirement. Most employees wanted more, but considering the situation with GM and Delphi and the losses the company has had, it might help them become solvent again, even though, the company should be looking at engineering info and marketing and pricing.

The Politics of Everything

When you're twenty years old and have just landed a good job at GM, politics don't mean much. In fact, you really don't care about that kind of thing. It's girls and money that are important. It was 1977 when I was hired, and the only thing I remember is that gas was cheap—about sixty-nine cents a gallon—and I was making more than my dad at GM. He had been an engineer, and he had decided to go a different way—broadcasting. He worked in sports at WPHM in Port Huron. I had gone to Central Michigan University but hadn't learned much. Jimmy Carter had beaten Gerald Ford for president,for whom I had voted for. For that matter, I thought that politics was boring. Oh, how wrong I was! Politics makes the world go round. I made more money when a Democrat was president than I ever did when a Republican was in office. Just look at your W-2s to find out. Most people wanted to make a good living, but when the Democratic Party went too lax, then the Republicans would take over. I mean everything—the Congress and then the Oval Office. It went back and forth. President Reagan took over in 1980 after the Iran hostage crisis. I got laid off in 1981 for the longest duration of my career. Interest rates soared to 14–18 percent for mortgages and the end of assuming them at lower rates as the banks got paragraph seventeen added to the mortgage, which meant they could put a due-on-sale clause on every mortgage. Reagan won again in 1984 as everybody was back to work and the economy was beginning to roll. Interest rates fell back to 9 percent and the retirees were still getting more for their money than that because they were locked into five-year CD rates. In 1987, the Berlin Wall fell, which meant that there would be freedom for the people of Europe who had been under Russian rule since the war. George Bush was elected in 1988 due in large part to the fact that the economy was going well. "No new taxes!" was his slogan. Desert Storm takes place after Saddam Hussein tries to overtake Kuwait. We decide to invade. No casualties. Iraq pulls back. Bush runs for re-election but is defeated by newcomer Bill Clinton, from Arkansas. He is different. "Slick Willy," they called him. And he was. However, I made more money than ever during his time in office, as the economy was doing great. Then came the dot-com era and the beginning of trouble in the world. President Clinton didn't do much around the world to stop the beginning of terrorism as we know it today. Scandal was the word of the day. However, the UAW still supported him for re-election, and he did win, due in large part to the Republicans putting up Bob Dole, a tremendous senator who didn't show up until he became a celebrity on the Jay Leno show after the election. Had he shown this side of himself earlier, he might have won. After re-election, the Republicans tried to impeach President Bill Clinton. Either way, the union stood behind their man. Then came the biggest election of my lifetime—George W. Bush and Al Gore. Bush wins by getting enough electoral votes. Florida becomes the key state. Jeb Bush is governor of Florida. They're brothers. It must be in the stars. Thank God for George W. Bush, one of the bravest men I ever voted for. My president had the biggest shoulders and strongest heart during 9-11. Sept. 11, 2001 shall live in infamy, for everybody felt that impact. The president did everything he could, with the exception of capturing Osama Bin Laden. Our nation is a kind nation that doesn't want to harm innocent citizens or create chaos. We believe very strongly in liberty and justice for all. President Bush was elected again. This time the Democrats put up John Kerry. Nice guy, but too much baggage. In 2005, we are still in Iraq. Oh yes! We invade Iraq to defend our country from weapons of mass destruction which weren't found. Sales slip in the U.S. The economy is doing okay except in the rust belts. They didn't support Bush anyway. Politics! I get it! I find out that GM is about to run on empty. Last year that matters: 2006. GM has a plan of recovery: get rid of the legacy costs and the older workers by buying them out of their contracts by offering them a golden handshake of $35,000 if you have thirty years or more with the company. People fall through the cracks. Who are they? The workers of 1977. The majority of them had to work at several different facilities and probably don't have 1977 seniority, but 1-7-85 seniority because of the OGM of 1977. This is corporate wide. Bummer for them, right? Twenty-nine years and they don't get the bonus of $35,000 even though many of them kept this company from going under. You say, "Well, they have to have a cutoff date for the bonus." Why? Because that's the way the UAW wanted it to be. After all, the majority of the 1976 employees hadn't had to leave their plants, and therefore they would be more familiar with leaving. Of course, they had the best jobs that wouldn't be replaced, and the 1977 seniority employees wouldn't be able to get them any way. Appointed people were mostly 1976 hires or older. International reps Were hired in 1976 or earlier. As a 1977-hired employee in 2006, I feel that I paid the same amount of union dues to this union and that I deserve the same treatment. The answer is that they just had to cut it off somewhere. Politics! Who will lead the next revolution? Where will the jobs come from? If you look at the reality that the unions are getting smaller and therefore less influential in the political arena, then who do you suppose will lead the middle class to prosperity? Not everybody should go to college. Some people are just as smart to learn a trade like welding, electrical work, plumbing, or die setting. You get the idea. Since when does America want to give up on the young? Without the united effort of my forefathers of 1937, I never would have been able to earn the type of living that I was blessed with. To them I offer my greatest apologies for not being able to return the favor to my children. It is all about college. Remember, some of us are supposed to be Indians. We can't all be the chief. Like all history, this situation has an opportunity to repeat itself. One last note: The international union has done a remarkable job up until this date in taking care of the rank and file. I'm proud of the Douglas Frasers, the Owen Biebers, the Steven Yokiches, and the future of this union. Let their ideology live on.

Union Politics:

I never really cared for politics and really never knew much about politics until I found out that I couldn't run for an elected position because the union didn't tell me about the fact that I had to apply for the out-of-work credits. I was considered in default on my union dues even though I wasn't getting paid by the union or GM at the time. How can that be? This was something made up by the union people to keep the younger members from creating a coup to topple the region. This happened in 1979, when I tried to run for financial secretary. They said I couldn't be on the ballot because I hadn't paid union dues and was delinquent. Please! Nobody told me I had to keep up on my dues. Politics! Howard Hodges, a longtime secretary for the union, was in power, and he didn't want to lose to a newcomer. He did eventually. I didn't get to run, but someone else won the spot. I made a difference, though. We had over 350 or 400 people from our plant at the union hall for the explanation of the out-of-work credits. Michael Bennett was the current president and he couldn't handle the situation, and the crowd was restless. Do you see some common ground? No! They stole the opportunity for the young people to make a difference. We never forgot that! They took the microphone out of my hands in front of many Local 326 dues-paying members. A sad day! I only worked in Flint V-8 for a short time, but it was long enough to know that their union was tight. In fact, they really didn't like the fact that I was from a different plant and that I might go back. The rank and file there was very dominant. Not a very educated bunch, though. They were a typical group of thugs trying to stay in power. Eventually, they were toppled. They made lots of mistakes.

Back to Coldwater Road, but no running for office. They had me stuck in a bad position. I was one of the lowest employees in the plant, and I had very little leverage. Lots of luck. Most of us didn't know from one week to the next whether we would be working or getting laid off again. It was a nice time to be working at GM. Roger Smith, with his plan of attack, hadn't announced yet what he would do. Laid off again! It was 1986; I waited to go into the pool. You had to sign up then. If you didn't sign up, then you would be passed by. I waited until the coast was clear at Flint Assembly, which was probably one of the hardest working plants, and I didn't want to go there. I get picked up at Metal Fab instead of Auduburn, which was where I wanted to go. It was a unit of the Local 659—greatest local of them all, the sit-downers. Jack Brown, shop chairman, greets me. Didn't realize how much influence he had at the time. Everybody adored him. He was tough and got it done. If you were right, then you were right. He became president in the next election, and Jim Stevens took over. He was smooth—not nearly as flamboyant as Jack, but just as smart. Maybe a little slick. He delivered! Jack and Jim went into the international union and we were left with Tony Boone. Excellent bargainer. He got tied up into too much union work and lost himself for a while. His right-hand man took over, and he took an appointed job. Norwood Jewell became shop chairman. Talk about slick; you could cut him with a knife. Nice guy, though. Nice guys don't always win, but in his case it worked for him. Right place, right time. Norwood took us out on strike, and I'm proud to say he did it with pride. That strike of 1998 was huge in the face of adversity. GM hadn't seen a strike since 1970. I don't remember that one; I was only twelve. Although we found out later that the international union had a lot to do with it, it didn't matter. Norwood became an icon. Later, Tony Boone ran again and was defeated. His time had come and gone. The strike had put a blemish on our plant, and we couldn't live it down. Norwood moved into the international union, and we got Tom Carahan. Tom was a veteran and also had been through the rough times. We elected him thinking that everything would stay the same, but he lost leverage and focus. He got caught leaving the plant on company time and also lost credibility with the membership. We lost jobs and opportunities. We elect someone new—a truck driver with no experience. He can't handle it and has a heart attack, or so it is told. The days of the union holding their own is over. Do what the company wants and maybe you'll get new work. Our plant had been guaranteed work from the strike of '98, and that is all we got. No new investment and no new work. Our union had grown weak. It's not entirely the fault of the union, but it is the fault of people in general. I want to be the boss. The boss has it too good. A lot of people along the way lost elections. The union shouldn't have groomed them for the times like these. They had wanted to serve. Instead they chose to squash the opposition, which is not good for the future. The union today has very little room for the experienced. We've all gone. I hope that the new membership can elect new blood. It's new blood that makes the union smarter and tougher. New ideas, new thoughts and new ways to deal with management are what they need. Good Luck!

What You Don't Know Can't Hurt You?

The most horrific CEO of our time, Roger Smith, would have consolidated the GM facilities and produced products that all looked the same, and to get rid of him, we had to give him a one-million-dollar-a-year retirement package. Ridiculous. If they can change my package midstream, why can't they change the big shot's? He made us smaller and less efficient. For one thing, we couldn't sell as many cars because he killed lines that made specialty cars. Should we have to pay a GM CEO one million dollars a year for life when the blood, sweat, and tears came from the workforce that have to attain thirty years of employment to get $1,500 per month plus surrey? Surrey is the supplement that Social Security will pay if the employee is sixty-two. One employee retiring for another thirty years wouldn't even get the one million dollars that Roger Smith gets, and that's not including the stock options that he has. Ridiculous! Robert Stempel was a good old boy who earned his right to be CEO. Great guy, but Wall Street didn't like him, and therefore he was gone way too soon—before he could make a difference. Jack Smith, as CEO, was a quiet fellow who handled things in the boardroom. He definitely was a leader. He brought the best out of the executives working for him. He also was blessed with a great economy. That always helps make you look better when your stuff is selling. Trucks were his thing, and it worked. America was in love with its trucks. Why? Lots of reasons. One is they still had chrome on them, and they were powerful. America loves power. Another reason is the fact that gas was cheap—$1.19 a gallon; even $1.39 wasn't bad. The trucks GM was building were beautiful. Great colors. They were also advertised well. They were versatile. They could haul stuff and were dependable and long lasting. In fact, GM rarely changed the design much—only about every eight or nine years. Profitable? Oh, yes. The most profitable product ever built only had a small cab with an extension with or without carpet. Finally, the bottom fell out of trucks after 9-11. Manufacturers don't sell as many trucks and SUVs now as they did then.GM has another huge money maker.lose sales. Why? Gas goes up due to the terror attack and the threat of more such attacks. Lots of workers are still driving these gas guzzlers, and the overtime goes away. A new CEO takes over—a young guy in terms of leading a company as large as GM. Rick Wagoner runs a tight ship, or so he thought. His leadership would see the end of GM holding onto 30 percent of the market. Why? The global market! NAFTA and the new CAFTA are in effect, leading to outsourcing, cheap labor overseas, and foreign competition on our own home soil. There are other factors as well: the inability to adapt quickly to market changes, such as the price of gas going to $3.00 a gallon; a political environment that wouldn't listen to the cries; and attempts to break or at least bend the union. Delphi says they can't make it without concessions from the unions, yet they continue to work. They say the contracts are too rich. Please! They hire a guy at Delphi to break the union. He says that he'll work with the union if it's possible. He's cocky and very brassy.The membership smell a big brew coming. Delphi flies for bankruptcy! Why? It can't afford to pay its workers wages that aren't competitive with the world. What? This is America, the land of the free, a place to make money and prosper. That's why everybody wants to immigrate here. Delphi wants to abolish the UAW contracts through the court system. Politics! President Bush does nothing, as he is preoccupied with the Iraq situation. Think about it: Republicans don't usually help the unions because they don't support them in an election. So if they are in power, they make it good for big business. I'm just saying! Look at their policies and their voting records. Democrats usually support the unions and their cause. The problem with the Democrats is they lost touch with the center of the voters. Most of us are independent when it comes to voting. I believe that each candidate shows what he or she is throughout the process. The problem with the parties is there is a lot of baggage that goes with each candidate. Where is the conservative Democrat—the one for the people and for the prosperity of all, a believer in what this country was founded on: liberty, justice for all, and God? Too much attention is placed on the importance of special-interest groups. Money is the king; re-election is most important. Think about it: wherever you live, chances are good that you've had the same congressman or congresswoman or senator you whole life. Change! Nobody likes it, but that is what makes the world go round and makes life interesting. Anyway, my feelings are that GM will survive, but that it will be much smaller, leaner, and quicker at quicker at changing with the market than it has been. Also, they will be profitable by 2008, mostly because they will have gotten rid of a lot of extra fat in the terms of people. Legacy costs aren't as expensive as they seem. For most of us, we won't enjoy what the Roger Smiths, Jack Smiths, or Rick Wagoners have, but we will know that we contributed to the success of this company with hard work, the dedication of coming to work in snowstorms when other people didn't, working in sweltering heat of well over one hundred degrees for hours to make a buck, dealing with bosses who didn't like us because of our looks or the color of our skin. My hat's off to the men and women of the '70s who kept the tradition of GM alive and put forth the effort to make it to the end of their careers. Most of us would have liked to have our children continue the legacy, but the politics are not in our favor. Our leaders let this happen. Greed! I'm proud of what I've accomplished and the acquaintances and friends I've met along the way. I do not know color or race or gender. If I've learned anything at GM, it is the fact that we all are different and we all go home to different families and situations that make life interesting and wonderful. I thank GM for giving me the ability to raise a family and to learn what it's like to live in different cultures, as well as the opportunity to understand that you have it one day, and one day it is gone. The recipe for success is not measured in a day, but in the long hours on the line spent improving, and in knowing at the end of the day that you made a difference. I wish only the best to my comrades, whether they are management or hourly. Your struggle will be rewarding in the end. We just need to be able to have better politicians taking care of this America—land of the free!

A Few Days after the Election of 2006:

Change is coming! There has been a shift in power in the legislature. Control is in the hands of the Democrats for the first time since 1994. Will it make a difference? Only time will tell.

Terror Attack: September 11, 2001

I remember where I was when the news came on the radio five minutes before 9:00 a.m. It was just before break, which I was looking forward to. It seemed like a very typical day, and everything in the UW cradle cross-member area seemed the same. But it wasn't. Tim Duplanty was running the end of the line, and it was getting backed up as he listened to the radio. I asked what was going on, and he said that the twin towers in NY had been hit by two planes that were hijacked by terrorists. We all stopped and just waited for more news. In fact, I went upstairs to the cafeteria and watched the horrific moments that followed on CNN. You see, I had a thirty-minute break, and for the whole time, I sat and watched the situation unfold. It was as if life stood still for that time. The plant was buzzing. What next? I went back to my job but really couldn't do much. A few minutes after we had gotten back to work, Tim said that another plane had hit the Pentagon and that there were still a couple more in the air. Almost all the employees in the UW cross-member area stopped working for a while. Barry and I were far enough ahead in our work that we could take a few moments to reflect. Keith, who was next to us, stopped working as well and came to the back, where I worked, and said, "What do you think you're doing?" As usual, Barry said something ridiculous.

Barry and Keith were best friends, and had been for a long time even before I knew them. We were all stunned and very upset. Not to mention the fact that our boss still wanted us to meet our usual production goals. My boss was a black man whom I really liked and learned to respect more and more for deflecting criticism and problems. I had earlier had run-ins with this boss, but had worked through them. My father told me that this guy was probably the best boss I ever had and that maybe I should tell him so. I did. Guess what? Life got easier. One of the most difficult things to do is to admit that you are wrong, and I had a tough time doing this, because most of the time the things that management would tell us to do would not be right. I mean just that it wouldn't be right for the situation, but they had to follow the leadership—superintendents who didn't have a clue as to how things work during a day on the job—any particular job. They knew their jobs, but not the floor. This boss had been overlooked way too many times by his peers. He continued to do a great job and deflect criticism. If he hadn't had a wife and a daughter in college, he might have looked to get out sooner. We would talk about our children and we would talk about sports or even the stock market. There was no color barrier; we were just people trying to do the best we could with the cards we were dealt. Getting back to the day, we started to get back to work after a while, but we just couldn't get the numbers we needed. My boss said that what we had done would be good for the day. We had only completed two-thirds of the work required, but he had compassion for us and the rest of the country. We retired about a half hour early and went up to hear any new news and waited to go home to our own loved ones and hug them. His name was Henry, and I never forgot him. When I think of bosses, I have to mention one of my few favorites, Larry Polzin, who was a former line worker himself. He expected perfection and he got it. Basically he told you, "do what is expected or else." *Else* meant getting a paper written on you and eventually time off for subpar work. I was a welder in the C-cradle at the time, and our cradle was the best in the world, at least we thought so. We had 100 percent efficient and we were on time or early. Chuck Putney also was a great boss. He was a little kinder than Larry, but still expected excellence. Both ended up going back to hourly jobs to finish their careers because they couldn't get what they wanted. This was another lost opportunity for the company. Another boss I really liked was Jim Corkran, a previous security guard who had to become a foreman due to the restructuring of GM by Roger Smith and co. I worked for Jim during my last years, when I became a fork truck driver. He was a tough-nosed kind of guy with an awesome personality. He made me smile, and he was fun to work for. Lots of times, he would ask me to do things that weren't my job, but I would do them to help him get ahead, and he appreciated my efforts. That's all you can ask for. He was a cool character. He had a completely bald, shaved head. We would talk during breaks, or even during the day, and he was solid and confident—the kind of boss that everybody could look up to. He also got looked over by the upper management. If there was any rhyme or reason to GM, it was that they were unpredictable. Just when things were going smoothly, they would change your boss because they thought that the boss was getting too close to his or her workers. I thought that was what the team concept was built on—trust! In fact, my last two years were the best I ever had at GM, because I finally figured out that I could do more for myself than get into a battle over who would do the work and who would be upset if I didn't do it—including the union. I rarely, if ever, called the union rep unless it had to do with my vacation time off, which rarely was turned down until I became a truck driver and had that stupid 1-7-85 seniority date that I was saddled with through my whole career. Gypsies! The international reps had no idea how bad that date had become, nor did they care. Our international reps had become very affluent with their separate pension and their tight little caucus. It's funny that we still didn't get any respect from the local union reps even though we had paid union dues for over twenty-nine years and had provided them with such a good living. I figured it out, along with the rest of the area hires, when the offer to make a break and hopefully keep this company solvent came up. *Get out! Take the money and run.* Although I wasn't able to get out due to my disability, many did, and good for them. I think GM could do it again and include the 1977s. It's only fair. Besides, then they could restart this company. Sometimes it is better to regroup rather than dissolve. GM will be solid again. The upper management now in place has a focus that hasn't been seen since the days of 1977.

Saddled With an Injury:
September or Early October 2001.

I was working on a job I was very familiar with, but wasn't supposed to do unless there was an absence or illness. After lunch, we would normally only have about an hour or a little bit more to spend in the UW frame area. We weren't allowed to get done any earlier, unlike in the late '80s or early '90s, when we would reach production quotas every day and then be done. In this case, there was no bonus time unless you created it and unless everybody worked as a team. Working on the front of a system that was designed wrongly from the beginning, I continued to put part after part into the fixture and then clamp them up. I worked with a partner whom I hadn't worked with much before. I reached for a rail that was on a hook on a conveyor. The part wouldn't come off the hook, and it was getting closer to going over the area where it would break the hook off or shut the line down. If the line shut down, we wouldn't get done for another hour or two because the production we were ahead would be used against us. The union had given that away at the last contract. I turned and my knee didn't. My foot was planted on a rubber mat. I blew my knee out right then and there. It killed me, but I retrieved the part and kept right on working so the line would keep moving. I placed the part in the fixture and proceeded to weld the part. I called over the boss, who had been in the area, watching, and said that I had a problem. This short black man who also was a preacher on the outside, said he would try to find someone to take my place. A half hour later, he did. In the meantime, I continued to do the job and work under pain. When I finally got relieved, we only had twenty-five or thirty parts to go. I went down to the hospital and then got a little treatment, but no doctor was in. The nurses were always great. They were helpful, and most of the time, cordial, unless they'd had a bad day. We all have those. It took almost a year to get GM to admit that there was an injury. I had a tear in my right knee. I had surgery and it was a success. The surgeon said that I would be back in two to five years depending on the job I did. If they put me back on the same job, then it would be two years. GM paid for my surgery and then told me to go back to work and put me on the same job. Two years later, I went back in to see the surgeon. No tear yet. Actually, I went for a consultation. Next year, I had moved on to a different job—fork truck driving—and I started to feel pain again. Went into the doctors office at the shop, but they only took X-rays and couldn't find a problem. Got permission to have an MRI done and oh yes, there was a tear in my right knee again. Delayed surgery until after the first of the year. Elected to have surgery again. Went in on Jan. 17, 2005. Out for only five weeks this time before they said I was ready to go back, and I actually didn't feel that bad. Normally it would take eight weeks to recover fully. Third day back, *crap!* Getting off the truck and back on was not feeling right. In fact, the knee never felt the same from the third day after I came home from having the operation. What! Well, you see, GM had taken out all the wood floors and poured cement eighteen inches thick in its place. I couldn't walk on the floors that well. Anyway, it took me three weeks to see my surgeon again, as he was in the Bahamas and Florida.

I Finally got in to see the doctor and he couldn't believe it. I couldn't bend my knee or squat. I got a restriction that limited my workload. GM had been getting out of the Cripple Creek work for a long time; they said they had no job for me and put me out on medical. My restriction was for three months. No rehab at all. Just rest. Then, when my doctor found out they had released me from the restriction, he couldn't believe it. He didn't know they were doing that. I went back after three months, and my surgeon said that I would need another twelve to thirteen months of the restrictions. They said again that that was unacceptable and they released me to medical. Out again till next year. This would make it 2007. I had missed out on the early-out packages although they wanted me to retire without the golden handshake that the majority were getting. I declined. Finally, I decided that my knee wasn't improving, and needing some closure to this situation, I asked for retirement through the disability claim form. I needed a doctor to fill out the paperwork on my condition and say that it wouldn't get better. Called my surgeon, but he was out of town for a couple weeks. I dropped it off anyway. No response. I finally called, but they hadn't filled everything out due to the fact that the surgeon hadn't looked at it. I said "What?" Called my family physician. He's been my doctor for eleven years, but I wasn't sure if he knew everything or if GM would think that I was only using him because the surgeon wouldn't do it. Quite to the contrary, my physician is very well regarded, and he filled out the paperwork, and then my surgeon called in the next couple of days and said he would do anything for me. He also said that I wouldn't be getting better as I had osteoarthritis in both my knees and that they would continue to get worse. Nice! I'm only forty-nine, not quite fifty, with 29.7 years of service with GM. Would I fall through the cracks as so many others had before me, or would I be one who in reality gets lucky and is told by the company that they will take care of me? The company agrees! I can't believe it; after all, I still have a family to raise—a ten year old at home and a son in college. And might I add that he was just starting college.

Nonetheless, the paperwork and the phone calls caused much stress. One thing I will say about all of this is that I had the best work comp guy helping me through the process; he was named John Baringer. He was awesome. He deserved a raise. I hope he got one. He took care of my case very well and always had a kind ear. Thank you, John. I also want to thank my shop doctor, Dr. Donna Smith, for treating me well and following through on everything she said. The one part of the equation that I didn't figure on was that GM had somehow transferred all the retirement part of the business to Fidelity and EDS. EDS did the figuring on what someone was entitled to and Fidelity handled the transfer of funds. So talk about red tape; you had to have everybody on the same page. That takes time, even in this world of e-mails and high technology. It is still about work orders,One person can't take someone elses place ,let alone send out specific mailings. Signatures are needed.. Does this sound like something you wanted or planned to do? I've been to three plants and worked with many different personnel. The best of these plants was Flint Metal Fab, which meant working with Jewel Goff, a black woman who was not only personable, but also cordial. She helped me when others couldn't or just wouldn't take the time. Hats off!

It was a rough ride as I got used to not having certain amounts of money, especially the OT. I'm coming to grips with it now just because I have to. I really liked working. Maybe I didn't like all the politics, but I enjoyed succeeding in my job. I felt like GM and the Flint Metal Fab family had been abandoned. Let's face it, the big boys knew that the strike of '98 would help them, or it wouldn't have happened. As of this date—Friday Nov. 17, 2006—I haven't received my papers regarding my retirement. I expect to see them in the mail very soon. One thing about retiring it that all of sudden, the things that mattered and may have been a part of your life don't matter.

I'm disturbed by the way the American public has written the young and the talented off. I only hear from the trade magazines that the companies have too much burden. We wouldn't be having this conversation if it wasn't for that burden. Burden is everywhere, whether we look at the politicians getting a compensation package or the executives getting a huge bonus and retirement package. Let's face the facts; this is America. What it needs to be corrected is for the other companies to become part of the global economy and recognize the international union. The politicians need to understand that we all need to have health insurance and make a decent living. GM is a living legend, and with the talent it has at the helm, I'm confident that they will bring this company back. It won't happen overnight, but within the company. A couple marketing gurus will come up with something that makes this company rock. Consider this: If they hired more young people and they bought more GM products and talked about GM products like we did, then what do you think would happen? It is perception and what you can give back that counts.

Old Newsboys: Wanting to Give Back

I never realized what a huge impact one person could have on some young persons at Christmas. It is the year 2000, and I'm selected to help in the Old Newsboys campaign. Never had this opportunity before. I only got this opportunity through my good friend Danny Martin, who had been doing this for years. I would take the day off from GM and serve the Old Newsboys by selling papers on a corner in Flint. Danny Martin was the captain of the corner of Linden and Corunna roads. He really was a great promoter and friend of the Old Newsboys campaign. Dedicated! I only knew that I was to be there at 7:00 a.m. and that I was to sell until all the papers were gone. My first experience was really exhausting, but it was also exhilarating in light of the fact that we broke all past records for the sale. It started out very cold and stayed that way. It then started to rain, and it then turned to snow. The people of Flint are a very generous people. I witnessed young people give everything in their piggybanks, and many others, including many businesspeople, gave twenty and sometimes fifty bucks at a crack. Eventually, I could tell who would donate and who wouldn't. It didn't matter what they drove. It might be a Porsche or a Jag that didn't and an old van that would. For the most part, the people of Flint and its surrounding areas were generous. After all, I was standing in the middle of the road, waving papers! The drivers might have even bought at the previous corner, and yet they might still give their last buck. They rarely complained. It was one day and one time during the year for one cause that meant much to many. I enjoyed the experience of learning about the people of Flint. The next year, one lady bought us all hot chocolate and coffee from Tim Horton's on the corner. She never stopped. We kept bringing in more dollars, and although GM provided, they decided to cut the number of employees they would let go out to the corners on that day. It used to be eight, then it was seven, then six. I became the odd man out in 2004 and had to work a different corner. I worked the corner of Fenton and Hill—the corner that was the most productive. Only this time we did it with five people. I missed my friends harassing me to do better, but I still had a good time. We didn't do as well as we could have due to the rain and cold weather. The economic conditions were also turning against us. Nonetheless, the people of Burton gave what they could, and the people of Grand Blanc and Flint did also. They really came through every year. My friends Mike Cicilo, Scott Griffin, Danny Martin, Woody, and the rest of the gang came through every year. I understand that this year they don't have enough volunteers to work the corners due to the recent changes at GM. I hereby volunteer. I'm sure my friends would also. GM always paid us for this day, but I would do it anyway now that I see that it makes someone's life a little better. My father only found out about my community service a few years before his sudden death, but he always said that this was a special something I had, and he always bought a button from me. Buttons are what givers receive when they donate 20 dollars or more. He lived in Chicago. I used to go to the Owosso business community to get sponsors. I rarely got turned down. One of the greatest achievements we made was breaking the record in 2003 on the corner of Corunna and Linden when we brought in over $6,000 on one corner. Thanks to all who contributed and all who donated. I felt very blessed to have been a part of this achievement. Danny, the captain, really wanted to make this happen. We worked on this day until after three. We were frozen, but the kids had a nice Christmas.

Again the date of 1-7-85 becomes important. Why? Because this date would determine whether you would be able to get preference for a job or get an appointed job or get an opportunity to work for the kids in the Old Newsboys. That is what the deciding factor in everything was—seniority. All the people in power who had the authority were from the Flint Metal Fab plant. It was always a challenge to break in, and I never really did. Missed opportunity. Charlie Martin was the coordinator of the Old Newsboys for years, and he was an old caucus boy. He remembered the 1993 YOU campaign, and that is probably why I didn't get in sooner. Politics! See what I mean? So many people, so few leaders. I don't know who will lead the next wave of power.

Let's Talk About Friends:

Hey, we all have them. Some are closer than others, and yet we all need them. My first friend I met at Coldwater Road was named Dan Scollon. He was older than me, but had a great personality and lots of drive. I had lots of acquaintances at Coldwater Road. Another friend was Dan McMillan, and another was Danny Martin. Tony Vargo was another friend. Not to mention the people on different shifts that I worked. I had lots of fun at Coldwater Road, and I'm sure the rest of us did also. It was a great environment to meet people in no matter what shift you worked, as they would cross over many a time. The fact that most of us who had gotten hired in recently were under twenty-one made it even more interesting. Try working with people who didn't want to be there but whose parents got them the job and who were very good looking. I'm talking about the girls! They seemed to be everywhere—all about the plant—but mostly in departments nine and three. I worked third shift and loved it, because it was summertime in Michigan. I love summer in Michigan. I didn't sleep much. I used to get up by 11:00 a.m. and head to the beach. I would get home by 5:00 p.m. and sleep till eight or so and then eat something and do it all over again.

Anyway, it was tough to develop any relationship with someone, as we were always kept on the bubble at GM. You might work overtime one week and the next you might not. I did not see my family much during the first couple of years, which was my own fault for trying to make money and play the field. Well, I met a little gorgeous thing one night at The Light, a disco, in 1979. She was hot!

I had dated, but I had not found someone who made me think that way! She came from a good background with a mom and dad who were still together; in fact, her dad was union president of one of the locals at Consumers Power. I called him Boss. Her mom was very good looking, and I thought that these little women would always be attractive. Besides, I was infatuated with her. She was 4'9" and had attitude, like me. One of my favorite moments with her was when I was going with her and I had her come to one of the many softball games that I played for the union team. I told her that I would hit the ball over the right fielder's head, and I did. That impressed her. I circled the bases. We won the game, but more importantly, I won her over with that hit. She still is my wife today, over twenty-seven years and going strong. We kind of grew up together.

The funny thing is that a lot of us think that we'll find true love the next time or that we can't find the right one. In 1979, life wasn't that different. What was different was that we both were working and willing to take the risk, unlike people today. What's funny is that I still have friends I met in 1977. I am still in contact with Danny Martin, Dan Scollon, Toni Vargo, and many more acquaintances.

I live in Owosso, and have since December 1979. I moved here for the convenience of being closer to my fiancée, Amy. I had been driving out here every night for a long time. It was a small town. Homes were affordable, and the people seemed nice. I'm still here. Tom and Gary Shepard live here, and they have for a long time, too. We used to drive to Coldwater Road together. Coldwater Road was a great time. What made it so good were the people and the point of time in our lives and the excitement of getting a paycheck that we could live on your own without help from our parents. Of course, I had been on my own for some time, but the fact that I was making it was very significant. It allowed me to get married and provide for my family. Thank you, GM.

Dan Scollon lives in Owosso also. Danny Martin recently retired from GM under the buyout agreement. Good for him. Scully had to retire early due to an injury at another facility. Gypsies! See what I mean? We never had the same opportunity as the group before us, and the group after us will have to fight for their lives to stay in one plant. Toni Vargo is also retiring within the next month. Congrats to him. We were the last of the true diehards and the last of the Coldwater connection. We hung in there. We earned it!

I only wish that the things could have been a little better for our kids. Not all of our kids want to go to college or necessarily need to go. They might have a trade that they're good at. When people ask me what I will miss about the shop and Flint Metal Fab, I won't tell them about the fact that I was never able to get the job I wanted because of my 1-7-85 seniority date or that the union played politics with certain jobs or that I never got recognized for certain accomplishments. I'll tell them that I miss the opportunity to be productive and to make a difference and that I'll miss a few people, including management. They're all gone now, and it's up to the next generation to deliver. Good Luck!

Friends I'll Miss!

Gary Shepard and Tom Shepard are two brothers I used to ride to work with at Coldwater Road They stayed at Coldwater Road till the end. Gary and Tom both retired. Gary and Tom both had to relocate to Saginaw. Their plant eventually became Delphi. I think they worked at Steering Gear. Tom, who was my neighbor, left at the end of 2005. These guys were hard workers; at least that's what I remember.

Jerry Jones and Steve Gubansik were truck drivers in the end, just like me, but I definitely remember them as hard-working people who enjoyed coming to work. They would do whatever it took to make the company money, and we would have conversations about the turmoil at GM. They both had a few more years than me, but they never treated me like they were better; for that matter they would take lesser jobs so as to make my job easier. Not all the time, but enough for me to know that they were special.

Jim and John Sincisson were two brothers whom I worked with at Metal Fab. John was very quiet, but also very intelligent. I sold him a home years ago, and I think he is still working. Jim was always the one with information, and he was quite a character. I enjoyed his conversation. We all worked different shifts at one time or another. Jim liked third, and so did John. Jim and I would talk about buyouts. John and I would talk about the changes at the shop. Duane Vieau, was probably my best friend in the '90s and early 2000s. We worked together for a number of years. He was a good friend and great fellow worker. I got him interested in the 401(k) program. He really ran with it. We worked hard in the C-cradle area and the GM10 area. We both went on third shift together. He had a few more years in than me, and he retired in 2003, I think. I hope he is doing well. He lives in the Houghton Lake area.

Barry Barkawietz and Keith Ballom were both really hard workers whom I got to know when I went on first shift in 2002. Barry and I worked together on a two-person line. We also golfed together in a league. Keith worked next to us and used to come over and talk, as he was Barry's best friend. They even bought some land together up north. It's on the way to my cottage. Danny Martin, Scott Griffin, and Mike Ciccalo were the boys of Coldwater Road. Scotty and Mike worked in the same department in the late '80s in Metal Fab. We helped make the Metal Fab family. Danny was always around, but not in the same department. Danny was always concerned about everything. He had a kind heart.

Arlie Maxwell was a guy whom I worked with in different jobs but never really got to know until we got stuck together under unique circumstances. Both of us had worked in the welding areas. He had always had a better job than me because of his corporate seniority of '76. You see, he also was an area hire. Arlie was a quiet type of person until you got to be his friend. He then would open up to you. I always thought of him as distant, but that was far from the truth. You see, Arlie was into his own thing, and the shop was just a place to make money—lots of money. He never turned down OT. And neither did I. He was the breadwinner, like me. I never saw a guy work so much overtime. He would work twelve hours a day, seven days a week. He would tell me that his kids needed something and that he wanted to help. It finally got old, the overtime, I mean.. I also would work the overtime, but I couldn't do the twelve hours every day. I had to take a day that was just eight hours. I just couldn't do what he could do. One day in late 2004, he told me he was going to have surgery to take care of a problem. I asked what it was, and he told me he had a hernia that was bleeding and that it needed to be fixed. This is a guy who had just worked twelve hours a day a few weeks ago. I told him I hoped it worked out, and he told me he hoped to be back in late December, before the holiday break. He didn't tell anybody until it was time to leave. I knew one day beforehand, but I think the boss knew earlier than that. Still, he was a very quiet guy. We had worked diligently together for over five months, including OT. I did his job and he did mine. We were a team, and we never worried who was doing more or less. When GM talked about teams, that is what they should have meant. They didn't. They meant reducing jobs. That was what teams meant to them. Well, Arlie's surgery went well. He came out of it fine. While he was off, though, he had these issues. One day, while sitting at his coffee table just before 8:00 a.m., he had a seizure. The stove was on, for he was making something. The water boiled over until the pot was dry. He finally woke up and called a friend over from next door. They went to the hospital. Tests were run, and they found a brain tumor. It hadn't been diagnosed before; I don't know why. He wouldn't be coming back to work for a while. After testing and all kinds of things being done to him, they decided that they couldn't operate on this tumor and that he needed to go to Henry

Ford hospital for testing because they might be able to help him. He was told that he had about one year to live. After treatments at Henry Ford, his prognosis is better. He might be able to live for another two to five years. GM retired him under disability one month after all the documents were turned in. What a turn of events. A guy who used to work all the OT. He was just like me, and now he may only have twenty-four months to live. Scary!

The two truck drivers who used to do the shuttling from one plant to another are now disabled. It's funny, when you think of it; both of us had worked so hard for years welding on the line, and once we got jobs that the people with higher seniority normally got, we didn't get to enjoy the benefits of seniority. Why? The number one reason is the fact that the blasted 1-7-85 has held us back for over six years. Most employees get good jobs after twenty years, but not the gypsies. That would have been 1996, and we sure didn't have the opportunity then. They let Arlie retire this year under total and permanent disability. I will be going to see Arlie soon, and I will talk of the good times. You see, Arlie was only forty-eight. I'm sure I have missed many of you, such as Lloyd and Fred, Danny Miglan, and Duane Yaklin, to name a few, but this could go on and on. The one thing I want you all to remember is that even though we weren't in a war for our country, we were, in effect, in a war for survival of the union, and we did make an impact. We paid our dues and we made a difference. Most of us will enjoy our retirement, but don't wait until there are no glory days!

2004–2006

A trend develops between getting a good job and the end of an era. First things first, I finally get out of the welding group and land a job in the fork-truck-driving group. And I can hold first shift. First, though, I have to go back on third shift for a period of thirty days before I am eligible to put in for my choice of shift. It is June when I land this opportunity. I went through two weeks of training and testing on first shift, got my license, and then it was changeover. I had the next two weeks off for changeover and then two weeks of vacation, which had been approved by my former boss in March, thank God. I never would have gotten this time off if I had been in the group—if I had been a truck driver, that is. This group was for the high-seniority employees, who were mostly men in their forties and fifties, with the occasional one in his sixties. It still came down to plant seniority and the fact that I had 1-7-85 seniority with OGM time of '77. That put me on the bottom of the totem pole as far as getting any good job within the group, so I learned them all. Didn't complain much unless I felt I was being abused. That really wasn't often. I learned to work with all the truck drivers on all the shifts, as we would work overtime every other week—mostly Saturdays and occasionally a Sunday. Even though I took a fifty-cent pay cut, I was making more cash with the overtime. I also wasn't on my feet, and my knee had been bothering me. Another reason for the opportunity to get out of welding was the fact that GM didn't need as many welders now that they were getting out of the frame business as I knew it. Lots of welders were doing different jobs, but most chose line work. Lost was the comradery of the welders and what went with it. Tough group. Hard workers.

Now we were just individuals among the many in a line job, in a group, and in a team concept. That's right, I didn't want to join a team. That was a big reason not to go on a line. The company was pushing the team concept on the line workers and the union, and they were eliminating jobs. Jobs for inspectors and checkers were going away, and the line worker had to do it. Repairmen were also at a minimum. You did it right the first time or you would stop the line and throw out parts that normally would be repaired and fixed. They might have had a couple dimples in a couple of spots. I thought that we became the top scrap producers. Meanwhile, the aluminum frame was producing world-class quality. It was the only frame we had left, and yet the production of this work was very low due to the fact that we only built this frame for a couple of products. The Grand Prix and the Buick Lacerne, or was it the Lacrosse? It used to be the Century, but the name had to be changed. Why? Outdated!

Were the Riviera, Park Avenue, Lesabre, Eldorado, Deville, Eighty-Eight, Ninety-Eight, and Cutlass all outdated? Hell, the Cutlass was the number one nameplate for years. Eldorado signified class. GM was trying to reinvent itself, but for what? Would you really rather have a Buick? Oldsmobile was the fireball eight, and the Cutlass always had the 350 rocket motor. Sweet!

What is Saturn? Another Roger Smith dream. Create something different and create a legacy.

Most of the guys didn't do much in the participation of the team concept except complain about their co-workers. This was just what the GM salary wanted. You can't teach an old dog new tricks. GM insisted that this would make us more competitive and therefore more profitable. Wrong! You make money with styling and recognition from the public. GM could have gotten the number one nameplate back at any time with the right marketing. It's not just pricing. Look at what we pay for trucks. Their prices are ridiculous considering there isn't anything to putting a box on the back of them. They look good to us. Styling! Why did we buy Camaros and Firebirds and Monte Carlos? They looked good and were fun to drive. SUVs are fun to drive, but they're not the old Monte Carlos of the early seventies.I owned a 1974, blue with white landau top, white bucket swivel seats, blue carpet and a good looking dash. The car still got twenty miles per gallon on a trip to Chicago. Rally rims, chrome-crank roll-down windows. I loved that. When the car was off, you could still roll the window down. Sounds like old school. It is! GM forgot their roots! The rank and file supported us the whole time. We were not a team or a concept; we were individuals who worked like a crank works on a motor. Sometimes you need a little boost, but instead of changing the rules, they should have inspired us. The squeaky wheel gets the grease. The union couldn't stop their persistence in having work rule changes that the wall street people insisted needed to happen even though they never stepped foot in one of our buildings. They didn't strap on a helmet and weld over 2,500 perfect welds every day. Bean counters were running the store now. They wanted us to be like Toyota, but were not Toyota. Toyota isn't perfect, but they have a plan and they stick to it. How long have they had the Corolla or the Camry for that matter? It's about perception. My perception is that we have to do what we're good at, and that is building and designing the best product for the masses. If you think that building a niche car is going to make you money, then you're going to have build a lot of them, and that costs money in technology and engineering. We are becoming a people of two classes, and the class that would like to buy a new car with a warranty is buying a used car. They have to; it is not because they want to. The big shots say everybody wants automatic features like power windows and locks. They say people want leather seats or very plush seats. Give the American people a product with the basics in a midsize car that gets twenty-five miles to the gallon and has the kind of power needed to pass. Put some chrome back on the vehicle and a little bit of flair. Make it like the Buick Regal of the early '70s or the Chevy Nova of that era. Include chrome crank-down windows. Design a coupe, or a hardtop; add a vinyl top and some detail. Make them different, but the frame could be the same. Inside, add a little detail to the trim of the seats, such as two-tone vinyl and an ashtray. The ashtray might hold a bunch of quarters instead of cigarettes, but let the owner decide. In any case, I think the workers were stuck in a situation that they didn't know how to get out of until one day after many quarters of losses by GM. The bean counters decided that they had too many people. These people were the life blood of the company, the ones who bought their products, the ones who helped sell their products to their families and friends.

Now the last of the true GM diehards are leaving the company because they don't want us. It's true. They only want to manipulate the new and temporary workers to their way of thinking. Unfortunately for them, the most loyal worker is the one who is leaving and was with you for thirty years or more. Good times and bad. We sucked it up in 1982 when another blunder happened, and then again in 1990. "It must be the guy on the line making us lose money; cut him." Not! The only thing that wasn't right about the buyout thing is that they didn't include the 1977 workers—the last of the gypsies!

Finding Your Place Among the Many—
Friday December 8, 2006

It's the holidays and it's time for the Old Newsboys campaign. I'm out on disability and the newspapers and the TV talk about the lack of people helping out in the campaign. I never realized how much we helped out. The union and management helped out a lot with fundraisers all year long. The biggest day, of course, was the day and afternoon that the Old Newsboys stood out on the corner and collected money for the children of Flint and Genesee County. I did it for the last five years, but not this year, and I can tell you that I missed it. I missed the friendly faces in the morning. I worked the busiest corner in Genesee County—the corner of Linden and Corunna roads. It is also the most dangerous corner, so I've been told. Didn't mind much, as the drivers were usually very observant. Occasionally, we would get someone in a hurry. During my second year there, we broke the record for the most money raised in a single day in one location. It snowed and was very blisteringly cold, but the guys stayed out there for the kids. People appreciated the fact that we were not pushy, but were just pushing papers for the kids. The union reps would bring us coffee once in a while, and donuts, too. They were donated, I'm sure, from the best donut place in the world, which is called Donna's Donuts. The cream sticks are to die for. I had a great bunch of guys to work with. Danny Martin was the captain, and I also worked with Scott Griffin, Mike Cicalo, Woody, etc. I was the youngest member, and when things got tough, GM cut one or two members off each corner, and I ended up on Fenton and Hill road. That year—my last year, 2005—Fenton and Hill was the top producer of money for the kids. I still missed the boys of Corunna and Linden. We made that corner. I missed not going to that corner this day, and I still hope they did well. I tried doing the Salvation Army bell-ringer thing, but it just wasn't the same. There is something special about having one day, one time, and one mission.

The funny thing is that Danny and I were so inspired that we even got businesses to donate to our corner during the year we broke the record. It takes dedication and inspiration.

At this time, I'm still not retired, even though GM wants me to be. Paperwork. I was supposed to retire on December 1 according to the last time I talked with the GM services center; however, now it is going to be Feb. 1, 2007. The reason is that I needed to give them sixty to ninety days' notice. If you remember, that was in September. The bottom line is that every day you don't retire is another day that they don't have to pay you for what you've earned. I also was told to get with my benefit rep the next time and finalize the process. I will be setting up that day real soon. That will be an unusual day. Perhaps it will be the last day I step into the plant as an employee. The days seem to have passed by this year without my giving much though as to the rest of the members of the plant. My mind was preoccupied with the other things, and the fact that many of my friends have signed on the dotted line to end their careers with GM through the buyout offer also contributed to this. It's like a displaced family. There is a lot to remember, and much has been forgotten. When you've put thirty years in with a company, you've got lots of memories—some good and some not so good. My wife always told me that you make an impact on the lives of everyone you touch or live with. I hope that this is true. From the beginning to the end, I always tried to do my best at GM. I didn't need someone telling me to do better, and most of us didn't. What we needed was someone to tell us that we made a difference in the way the company looked, the way the company operated, and the way the company made money. Long live GM and the hard-working people that make up GM.

What to do now? Patronize your company. I'm sorry to hear that GM is getting out of the van business. I think that they just couldn't break in. What they need is a product that will excite the masses. It's no different than a number-one single on the charts or an iPod. GM needs to take a chance on one of their young engineers and let it flow. Not everybody wants a suburban. The M-van, as it was called, had everything except new styling. It ran for twenty years on the same frame, and it also was all-wheel drive. I need a new one, but they quit making them in 2005. My family has grown but not left. I have owned five of these vehicles and will try to buy another one next year. They are dependable, reliable, and still handsome looking. The thing with some of the other designs is that the back-row passengers' feet are too close to the floor. We looked at them, especially the Tahoe. It is gorgeous looking, but there is no room for the feet unless you like to ride with your knees in your chest. Listen to your kids; they're the future—not that you're not. Be productive in whatever you can. Explore the country. Find the sun!

Find The Sun!

When you've worked in the factory for thirty years and then you are let out, you kind of feel like a kid again. The exception is that you have certain responsibilities. Maybe a mortgage, maybe college for your son or daughter, or maybe you are lost in what I do now.

Take a deep breath. Most everyone has been there, only now it's your turn, and you aren't ready. Most of us aren't, and that's okay. There are classes that can prepare you for the fact that you are now unemployed. What makes you happy? Well, we never got the chance to find out what really made us happy. Of course, we love our cars, but that is only going to go so far.

Find the sun! That doesn't mean pulling up and leaving the home that your kids grew up in, but it might mean finding something outdoors that you enjoy doing. We are the last of the dinosaurs to get a pension. The next generation won't be so lucky. The tide has turned, and the companies are going global. That means that, in the near term, they won't be looking after their workers like they used to. Elect someone who has your best interests now, not a vision that was in the past. If you think that the current people in Congress care about you, you're wrong. They care about getting elected again. Find the sun!

That means finding someone to enjoy life with and to live life to the fullest. Debt—we all have it. Our fathers didn't have as much as we have. Things weren't as expensive then as they are now, whether you look at college or TVs or cars. Find the sun! The fact is, many of us didn't see much of the sun while we were stuck in the middle of the plant, where the work absorbed much of our day. We're the lucky ones; we still get our chance. Make a difference in your son's or your mother's life. Whatever you do, don't just sit there and watch TV. Live life. Treat your retirement as an opportunity to do something for someone, even if it's for yourself. Find the sun! It might mean traveling, it might mean watching your grandchild, or it might mean starting a new career. The GM tap for retirees is barely, used and you might want to take the opportunity to learn something new. Find the sun! Go to a place that you thought was out of reach, such as Hawaii or California. We've been to Florida. I love it there. I don't like the congestion in Florida.

Most of us won't leave the great state of Michigan. We have found a home here and have lots of family here. I don't really know why we continue to put ourselves through this. Maybe it's the great outdoors: hunting, fishing, and snow. We have the best summers in the country. Our father lived here, and we've made our home here. As for me, I want to explore. I'm never going to be rich, but I'm not going to be poor either. I'm tired of only having three months of seventy-five-degree weather, and I like to golf. I will never give up my roots here in mid-Michigan, but at the same time, with all the things being the same, I'd rather be in warmer weather. Find the sun! Smile! Go to a different restaurant each week. Make an impact in your community. Volunteer. Above all, enjoy your time; you've earned it.

God Bless,
Leonard D. Lindquist

December 22, 2006—
the Last Day for the Many

It doesn't take long to feel the effects of the loss of all the experienced workers that GM has let go. It will be felt overnight. The first day of the New Year will be lost, and there will be many more.

The lack of hiring for so long has created a loophole, and the membership was stuck in the same job for so long that they lost motivation. They also had lots of experience and talent in their fields.

From the line worker to the tinsmith, it's a day to remember. The workers who help keep this company afloat after their heirs left.. Most of them had already gone, but some were always waiting for the golden handshake that they got today. I'm happy for them, but what took so long? We all have issues like starting over after a divorce or the loss of a loved one. Some didn't save for this day, and yet some never thought this day would come so soon. Hurray! Lots of people with lower seniority are saying it's great too, as they will now get the jobs that were supposed to be theirs long ago.

The date 1-7-85 will be implanted in my brain as well as the brains of many other employees. That date kept me from making more money, getting a better-paying job, and getting a better work schedule. Even my shift preference was affected. That whole thing was a debacle of the union. I'm still proud of my heritage and thank the union for its effort in providing me with a good-paying job. I'm just disappointed that they didn't do something about the date. They could have changed it anytime with the current contract, and that would've protected the rest of us. Instead, they elected to continue to let the sleeping giant rumble. Most of us gypsies were able to go today with the exception of the 1977s and 1978s who survived the transition of the eighties. I grew up with these men and women. Thirty years is a long time to be together.

Since I've been out this year, I've lost touch with the masses. I missed this day. This day would have been a day to reflect. Think about it. So many so fast, left the plants and perhaps unprepared. But you have to go. My Dad said that whenever an opportunity comes, you should move on, and he said that if the company is going through transition, then you should take their offer, because the next offer is usually not as good. The rumblings I'm hearing is that the next offer is not too far off. It will include the 77s and 78s. The kicker is that this time, if you don't take the deal, then you might lose some of those benefits you have taken for granted. Pension benefits with healthcare! That last word means the most to me. I still have a couple of children at home. I also have a wife. I'm getting older, not younger. Retirement! What does it mean? It used to mean a time to relax and enjoy everything God has to offer in life. To some, including myself, it means having an opportunity to do something enjoyable and being productive. Of course, that means making more money—probably not as much as you could make by working overtime, but doing something you love doesn't have to come with a big reward. Yet some will make more than they did in the shop. There were lots of talented brothers and sisters in there, and what kept us there were the benefits. The pay was just good enough to bring us back after a layoff.

Friends Who Left an Impact:

Eric Bristol was always quiet but had lots to say behind the scenes. I hear he is quite the carpenter.

Bob Rembitz was always on time and always ready to deal. He had an income tax business on the outside.

Jimmy Bennett left without saying goodbye when he went back to the Lansing plant. We used to ride to work together in the late 80s and early 90s.

Scott Jarred, one of my best friends to talk football with and the most dedicated member of YOU. He shaved his head so that it read "Y.O.U." on the back of his head. We need more of his type.

Big Ray and Al Ewell were a couple of the best basketball players from our three-on-three teams. We went into Owosso and won a tournament we shouldn't have. We were as determined to win on the court as we were to produce a quality part and do it on time at work. They made me good.

Johnny Johnson was one of the team of four and also a good friend who allowed me to help him in his real estate needs in the '90s. I'm sure he will be retiring soon.

Denny L'Hamedieau is a good friend who probably stayed. He moved into trades, and that's where the money is. He was an outstanding basketball player in high school, I heard. In the end all that matters is that you made an impact on some people's lives and that you were productive. I'm sure I'm missing many more, but that is typical of the way things go in life. You forget people by name, but not by spirit. I want you all to know that it was a journey that I wouldn't change for anything, and it was a great experience to remember. We were good. Very good!

Old Newsboys

The Flint metal fabrication plant was very dedicated to the Old Newsboys. We raised money throughout the year. We especially raised money during the holidays, and that started in late November. We would have popcorn sales. We would have hotdog and brat sales with chips and pop for lunch. We had the biggest electrician's raffle. This raffle raised so much money that it would pay for at least two hundred to three hundred kids' Christmases a year. Lots of prizes were won. I never won any, but lots of employees did. They did most of this on their own time. I saw second shifters on first shift and first shifters on second. Of course, there were always many volunteers from the UAW-appointed people helping out. Our plant used to raise at least 35,000–45,000 dollars per year for the Old Newsboys. This was something we all got behind. The plant also got behind the United Way. In the beginning, I felt that I was the only one not contributing to this program, so I started to donate time and money. I lived in Shiawassee County, and when they said I could donate to my community, I designated that my contributions went there. Either way, the United Way is a great program that offered many people a second chance to succeed. There was a time when the United Way was under scrutiny due to the lack of control at the top, but that has since changed. I've seen the development and growth. Still, the Old Newsboys campaign was the most fun. Something about getting out there and selling newspapers gave me a feeling of satisfaction. The guys were always pumped up, and the reception we got was fantastic. I'll miss it!

The Holidays: The End of the Year

Every plant that I worked at had a different type of end-of-the-year celebration, whether it was the parties that started after work, as was done at Coldwater Road, or the early days at Metal Fab, Most of the parties started after noon, or when lunch was. The work would be completed by then, and then the food and celebration would start. It was lots of fun, for the most part. People would let their hair down and relax. Young and old alike would be happy for the time to reflect on the past year and the things we had accomplished. Of course, the ladies always prepared the food, and the men just enjoyed it for the most part. The drinks were usually mixed and under wraps. Most everyone had a little something of cheer. There were always the stupid ones who would overindulge and then try to right themselves before it was time to clock out. Most of the time, someone would have to drive them home. That was especially true at Metal Fab. They were party people. It didn't matter what shift they were on, either. The most fun was on first shift. More people, including more salaried staff, would partake. They could relax. V-8 had a very small party for the line workers, as they continued to have to work, and they were only given one hour off. Greed! Most of the rank and file would get off, and they would have a good time all night. One thing I will say about the rank and file of all the plants is that they were generous with their money and their time. They were blessed. The membership gave their good tidings to all good causes. The company was also nice enough to allow the Shriners and whatever other groups the union and company agreed upon to raise money on company property during hours of operation. At the gates, there would always be people with a bucket to throw a dollar in for some cause. I praise the company for that. After the '90s, the plant at Metal Fab would also have a Kwanzaa week for the people that celebrated that occasion. The black leadership would put on a feast, and the membership also would get to listen to their music. They brought in a band and singers from the rank and file. It was fun.

Diversity

We had it and embraced it. Our group had come along way from the early days, when color was always a factor, to the time when we all got along very well and became one. We were not really a team like GM wanted, but we were together. There will always be conflict and discrimination, whether it is the white male who feels cheated or the black man or woman who feels he or she was excluded because of color. It is a fine line to walk, but when it is all said and done, the people of General Motors did a remarkable job growing in each passing year to come to this point. Christmas is a time of celebration and reflecting on one's life. The most important thing is to remember peace on earth and goodwill toward men. I think we demonstrated that throughout the years and got better at it. Metal Fab is best known for the strike of '98, but what I will remember are the many faces of the people of Metal Fab who made an impact on my life. Whether or not they know it, they contributed to the success of this company.

I missed the party this year due to my disability. I really would have liked to see the guys and gals one more time. You see, this is the last time that this many of us will be together. Retirement has a way of changing the things you do. You don't get up at the crack of dawn to prepare for work, and you don't worry about what the weather is going to be like, because you're not driving to work. I had lots of trying times when going to work in December from Owosso. I almost never missed work. Whether this was because of the money or just determination, I was there, and so were the majority of my co-workers. One thing I didn't like about the end of the year was the fact that GM changed the payroll system. We used to get two checks on the last day, or the last payday. They stopped doing this about five or six years ago, and so all you would get was your end-of-year check. We used to buy extra presents for the holidays with that money. My wife still bought them anyway. I just paid for them later. I prefer to pay in cash. My wife says that Christmas is for the kids, and I guess she is right, but we were all kids once. We haven't had any snow lately, and I don't think will get any in time for Christmas, but Santa will still make an appearance. He always does. Thank you GM. Thank you UAW. Merry Christmas to all, and to all a good night! Let it snow! Let it snow! Let it snow!

Too Young To Retire:

When is it time to retire? When is it time to hang up the shoes? Most all of us have contemplated this for some time. I'm talking about the baby boomers. We hear that we don't have enough money saved or that we don't have enough of this or that. I tell you that the best time to retire is when you feel comfortable with yourself. If you don't have a hobby or something to do, it will be pretty boring just being home and watching TV. Oh sure, that will last for a little while, but something will eventually pique your interest. Maybe you like golf, maybe you like the ocean and surf, or maybe you just like the freedom. Find something to do with yourself. Maybe politics! Why not? Get involved in your township or city. Make a difference. You have experience and you can get motivated. The shop was just a proving ground for you.

I hear that we are all too young to retire because we are just forty-nine or fifty or maybe a little older than that. Guess what? It might not have been our choice, but we will do our best with it. Some of us will become landscapers, and some will become roofers, yet some might invent something that everybody wants. Whatever it is, don't just sit there. You only retired from the shop, not from the real world. Opportunity awaits you. Explore.

You can make as much of your life now as you want. Spend more time with your children or grandchildren. Teach! Go back to school. Go to a gym. Find yourself again.

Hey, most of us don't want a full-time job again, but we would like to be productive. I keep getting this stuff in the mail saying I can put more money in my 401(k) on a catch-up formula. Well, I don't even know what I'm going to need to live on, so I can't rightfully decide to put more money away. Most of us were blessed with a company pension, and we will need that to help with the bills. Some of us put away some money in the earlier years, but most of us counted on the pension being there, and that is why GM has let us go—they have the money in there for us.

Is my house paid for? No! If you don't have to sell, then don't sell yet. The market will turn around, and then, if you have a lot of equity in your home, you can find a home that you can live with and buy it. Reduce your debt. Find a good realtor and stick with him or her. A good realtor will make you money in the long run, and he or she will create a lot less stress for you and your spouse. Buy a good car or truck. You're going to want to travel. After a year or so, you'll find yourself. That's when you make tough decisions, not before. You've got to figure out where you're going. Support your union and your former employer. They're still working for you even if you don't see it. One of my favorite things to do is watch the birds at feeding time in the morning. The all take turns being first, and that's what you should do, too. Be first when it's your turn to be first and then watch and listen. The music is pleasant to your ears.

Retirement Day—January 10, 2007

My retirement day was a day I'll remember much less than the day I hired in. I remember that they had grand or even subdued parties for them including many salary staff. Of course, I didn't get my just dues due to my injury and the fact that GM couldn't get the benefits portion of my retirement package right. That part is okay. They kept thinking that I was single all this time, and the fact is that I've been married for over twenty-six years, going on twenty-seven. I couldn't sign without protection for my best friend. They finally got it right, and so I've signed. According to them, I retired January 1, 2007. No biggie. They will get it right eventually. This company has so many checks and balances that it's no wonder they take so long to make a product work. I don't think they had this much trouble in the '60s or '70s. They just went with what was right. Lawyers and too much red tape caused this situation. Anyway, back to the shop. I did see my friends Barry and Ron. You remember Ron; he was now on a fork truck. Ron was the one who put me up in the air. Barry was the one I worked with for the last couple of years when I was welding. The plant had changed. It no longer seemed like my plant. The plant was not alive, like I remember it. It was very quiet. The people looked very methodical. I mean, they seemed very into their jobs and not into the people around them. The jobs were, for the most part, very easy but tedious. The new work that the plant supposedly had gotten had not arrived yet. There was a lot of wasted space. I ran into some of the older workers and wondered why they hadn't left too. They said they didn't trust GM to pay them their pensions, and also that the $35,000 wasn't enough. These were very confused people. These workers had said that the reason we all left was because we couldn't get better jobs due to our seniority. Of course, that might be it. After all, we had the 1-7-85 seniority date. That seniority date had held so many members from getting better jobs and making more money that the only alternative was to make a move. The 1-7-85 date has always been the catalyst behind our ability to become more productive. It was an alien. It was antiproductive, and it was the wrong thing to leave alone. This should have been addressed in every contract. The reason it wasn't is only in the hands of the international union. No more crying over spilled milk.

The UAW found a solution, and for the most part we took the opportunity. I commend the UAW for their effort and the effort of GM to find a solution to this global problem. Let's fact it, we are not in the '70s, but it might seem like it with the Iraq war seeming like Vietnam. It's not Vietnam. Iraq is a totally different situation because of September 11, 2001.

I ran into a few employees who said they would leave before the end of this contract. They had missed the deadline for the buyout but would still leave in July. I asked them why. They said that the contract this time would be tougher than ever in regard to holding on to our benefits and such, and they wanted to make a move south. Seems like everything is going that way. How much water do they have? These members just missed out on the buyout offer by a few months. They were '77 or early '78 seniority employees. Like I mentioned earlier, we stood to take the biggest hit either way, and the fact that we had worked at many different facilities for many years without complaint is amazing in itself. I worked at Coldwater Road from 1977 to 1986, but in between those years I worked at V-8 from November 1984 to January 1985, and then I went back to Coldwater Road. Why? Because that was my home plant, and that is where my seniority was. Then I got laid off again in 1986 after being on a temporary layoff for six weeks. It was supposed to be a rotation between the higher-seniority workers and the rest of the group, but somebody pulled the plug on that one. When I left in 1986, I didn't figure it would be four years plus before the corporation within Fisher Guide would need my services. I only found out when they decided to call me back. I had been working at Metal Fab for the previous four years, and I hadn't been laid off or even thought about being laid off. This plant had better management. It's too bad. Coldwater Road had some of the best people. They were not only hard working, but they also had attitude. With a good management team, they would've done great. In fact, they did; even when I got laid off, they produced the extra numbers that the company needed, and still the plant closed. That tells me something. If they want to close you and the politics needed to keep it open aren't there, then it's curtains. I want to buy GM. Rumor is the GM pep vehicle program is going away. That is too bad if it does. I realize this is an exceptional deal, and I've taken the opportunity to use it a couple of times. I'm going to be in the market to buy soon, and I am hoping that I'm retired so that I have the opportunity to purchase this way.

I emptied my downstairs locker and my locker upstairs that I used to use when I welded. There wasn't much in there. Surprisingly, there was a sweatshirt from when I worked outside. Truck drivers sometimes have to work outside to deliver their product to the semis. I'll miss it. I'll miss the friendships I had with the welders who worked very hard. I'll miss the friendships with the truck drivers who I learned from, and I'll always remember the friends I grew up with—the Coldwater Connection. We were very young, and now we're still not very old. Good luck to all of you, and may GM prosper.

The Dangers of Working at GM!

I never knew what to expect when I hired on in 1977, such as the toxic chemicals that I might be handling or the toxic chemicals that were in the air. I worked at Coldwater Road, which was known for die casting and chrome plating. They were very good at it. They had chemicals on the different dies and oils on the parts and fiberglass interior headliners. I mentioned the cleaning chemicals that were used to make the metal shine in the tubs at Coldwater Road I heard horror stories about stick welding in Metal Fab in the late '60s and even late '70s, which produced smoke so thick you could cut it with a knife. I was there in the '80s when we went to MIG welding, which was much cleaner. What I remember is that one time at Coldwater Road when I was sorting a gondola of parts, the truck driver went to pick it up and took my toe with it. My toe was busted, but not broken. It bled all over and I was off the job for a number of weeks. I saw many people get hurt by rushing to do their jobs. The next thing I knew, they were going to the hospital to get sewed up. Most of the older workers were smarter than the younger ones; they didn't work as fast, but they worked smarter. They probably had felt pain in their earlier years.

What you never expect is co-workers threatening you or more or less saying they would make you pay if you didn't leave their job site ready for them. One night at the end of my shift (which was morning) when I was working third shift, I was working my job in the UW-cradle area. It was about 6:00 a.m. The next shift—first shift—was starting to come in. The employee who was doing my job came up to me and said that he expected me to keep his job stocked up. Well, you can understand that at the end of the day or night you don't want someone other than your boss telling you anything. I told him that I would leave it the way I found it. That didn't sit well with him. Mind you, I was still working, and the work still had to be done. I planned on dumping another load into the baskets that I worked off of, but I would not do so much as to fill it to the top. That meant that the baskets would be less than half full. He came back about fifteen minutes later and said that I needed to leave him set for his shift. It basically came down to the fact that this area had gotten rid of a stock person and so we had to do our own stocking, which meant less time for production. GM was again thinking of cutting costs. I finally turned to this employee and said that I was not going to do what he wanted because my shift was over. He said that I was going to do it or else. Or else what! I'd had it. This was in 1996 or 1997. This smaller-built black man pulls out a knife and basically threatens me. I laugh at him. Not really a good thing to do. I grab a rail—actually a half rail that had to be welded together by the robot. It was quite sharp, but if we were going to go at it, I might as well have some protection. I told him to put that thing away or I would take it from him and it wouldn't be pretty. By this time there was plenty of company around as he made a spectacle of the situation. Needless to say, we both dodged bullets. You see, he retired recently, and believe you me, he probably never thinks of that day, but I do. Around the same time, maybe just a few months later, I was working overtime in the GM10 area. I was still welding, but now I was going to work first shift after working third shift all night. Twelve hours, they called it. Very good money. Hard to turn down. Well, lots of third-shift workers were working on this morning, as the company had fallen behind on this cradle. They had gotten rid of this cradle for the most part except for Chevy, which needed this frame for the Monte Carlo. I am assigned a job by the boss on first shift. However, there is an employee already on this job, or so she says. She is an extra person in the UW area on first shift who wants to do this job. I say, "I have been assigned this job, so you will have to be reassigned." She claims she has seniority. She has 1982 seniority from this plant, Metal Fab. I have '77 seniority, but from a different plant, and I have been saddled with this 1-7-85 date by the international union as an area hire. She wants this job and so do I. After all, it is a decent job—handling rails for the GM10 area—and I know it well from earlier years. She tells me that she will be doing this job or else. Not again! I tell her to go see the boss, as all the rest of the third shift has been assigned to the GM10 area. She says no. She starts to take over the area and says that I should go see the boss. I say the boss assigned me here. Finally, she stops talking and reaches into her purse and pulls out a revolver—a .22 caliber pistol that glowed silver, and it is loaded, or so she says. She says now without any conviction that she will be doing this job. Okay. I leave the area and go find the boss. I tell the boss that the job is filled with a first shifter and that I'll need to see the committeeman. A union rep comes down and says that I can't have that job. His name is Tony Prevost—a super nice guy, but not really the best person to call; after all, he is only protecting his people—the first shifters. I used to be more hard nosed about the situation, but now I figured I could just bump someone else out of his or her job. Nope, he says. The alternative is to go home. I elected to work another job. It didn't matter. I was getting time and a half—good money. I never told anybody about this, but years later the same black women worked together with me in raising money for the Old Newsboys. It's funny how people react when they are pressured. This gal also went on a mission to lose weight, and probably find her way to her goal in he union at GM.

Flying Dies:

The new way at GM is to have people who are working the line at GM also learn to fly dies. This job used to be a specialty, but now the company thinks that everyone should be trained to do it. Why? Because that way they can save on OT, reduce classifications, and so forth. Not a good idea. Some jobs need to be specialized. That is why I didn't want to work my last few years with some inexperienced die stager handling 50,000 lb. or greater dies. They fly overhead, and you'd better get out of the way. One spill and it's the end for anyone or anything in its way. Truck drivers are the next thing to be tested. We all had licenses, but once in a while they would let someone with experience on the truck and we would all go nuts. The biggest reason is safety, but the many truck drivers wanted to be paid. Truck driving is a closed group and that's that. I really think it should stay that way. Not everyone wants to jump on a truck that they're not familiar with and try to lift parts or a gondola or whatever. This is a skill. Plus GM always stresses safety. We had one hour a month of meetings on it. Anyway, when you read this part you'll understand why we get the wages we get. I barely touched on the dangers, but those were my experiences, not to mention all the rashes I got or the burns from welding.

Everybody Wants Your Money

I get letters from credit card companies and from financial institutions every day. They want you to give them your hard-earned money for a promise that they will deliver the goods. I mean, they promise to give you a great rate on your money whether it is borrowed or invested.

Since you are now retired, you will be asked to move your finances to their company. Your hard-earned money will be in the hands of somebody you don't know or someone that claims to be your friend. Your 401(k)? Your investments or your mortgage? You'll be getting less now, so watch out for the gamers. They're the ones who want to help but instead help themselves to the goodies. Why? Because you don't know and they do. "Invest" is the cry, and don't be shy. Diversify! That's the plan. Listen to your heart and watch what you buy in the next year. If you're a buyer in the pharmaceutical area, meaning you need a lot of meds, then invest in that business arena. You should never invest your whole portfolio. One of my favorite things to buy is candy corn. It might sound stupid, but I think that Brach's Confections is due for a huge jump in price in the stock market because they have the quality candy that is recognized. What they need is better marketing.

Remember, in a past chapter I mentioned retention of brand name and loyalty with marketing is essential to success? Buick would be the number one nameplate for GM if they would just market the product and bring back the Riviera and the Regal two doors only! I say make the Regal your idea. It might look something like the '73 or '74 models. It would have zip and the horsepower you expect. The Super Sport was an awesome product. Bring back the chrome on the car. Price this product under $20,000 and you'll sell all you can build. The only thing is, GM should change the exterior panels every two years and create an interior that people will love.

Money is a trading tool, and that is what it is good for. Keep some, but don't hoard it.

Your kids will want their own things, and that is why you need to enjoy what you've earned. With all the hype and press of the older workers retiring and the potential for growth for the younger people, now is the time to retrain and hire a group of young people who will have a future that is bright and full of the same things that the past workers enjoyed. Forget about the fact that you have to secure the past. The past is the past, and the future should be what the young want to make it. Political people should look to secure a solid manufacturing base in the U.S. If you give that up, then you've given up on this country. Make sure that you elect members of Congress who support the youth of this country and are aware of the plight of the aged.

Buy products that you think will help this country. I realize that GM and the rest of the big companies had to go to Mexico and overseas to compete, but at least they are still providing jobs in this country, and the fact that we allowed the politics of this country to get so screwed up is our own fault. Hiding behind a false platform and then voting a different way seems to be the way of the many in Congress. Once they are in, the pork barrels of life sink in. For instance, I've never seen what someone else would do in the senate in Michigan. I've always had Senator Carl Levin. That doesn't seem right. He doesn't even know me. It is not that he doesn't do a good job. It's the fact that he has many people who owe him something, and he will always call it in during an election year.

"Hey, remember when...?"

"I expect you to do this, or I don't think I can help you next time."

After thirty years, you've got quite a following. That is politics. That's life. It's not entirely what you know, but who you know. I know this: in order to get my money, you had better be looking out for my best interests and the interests of my family, my country, and my God.

Without one or the other, what does it matter? History will record it, but the impact you have on your fellow person is the most important. They are the ones lives that will be affected the most while you're here. I have a good church friend and just long-time friend who has had his son in Iraq three different times through the National Guard. That's tough! He's still there. He'll come home soon, and that will be a relief. His name is Scott Hoenshell. I played ball with him not so long ago. He is a terrific young man. I can't help but mention the fact that our son will soon be going off to college at Michigan

State University. He starts on Jan. 8, 2007, but will have orientation just a few days sooner. It's not like Iraq, but to my wife it's nearly that bad. I'm sure many of you have had to do this, and for some it was no big deal, but to us it is like another chapter or another page—kind of like this book. It is sad, and yet it is happy—kind of. It's an experience like retiring. What do I do now? It's always a new page, every day. Sometimes you would like to stop the pages from turning and the chapters from moving, on but you can't. Good luck!

Contract Time 1984

Owen Bieber, still the boss for the union, elects to take lump-sum bonuses in lieu of percentage wage increases. The membership loves it but doesn't realize that the sick leave and the life insurance don't increase. We only get a highlight package. Nothing is spelled out, but we have to vote on it. It passes. I vote against it. Nobody is listening. The international forms a new group called the Quality Network. The company and the union are jointly working together to form a common ground. Joint funds! Hey, where did they get the money for this? The union has more appointed people in every plant—at least two to three per shift per plant. That is at least fifty or so people getting paid to monitor what we do and try to improve it. We are joined at the hip. They also would be handpicked by the union for the most part. Sweet! All appointed jobs always went to the union caucus people and their friends. It's not what you know—oh forget it, you already know that. Another exciting contract change is that we get profit-sharing bonuses every year. Never had that before. That sounded good. The year is 1985, and Chrysler is doing well after their near collapse. They reward their employees some $5,000 to $6,000 plus in profit-sharing bonuses. Ford pays out on average $1,800 or so, and GM announces that they will pay their employees about one hundred bucks. They had another tough year with all the salaries and employees, so the amount must go down.

Of course, they had to start a new company called Saturn. That takes money, and in order to make money, you must make a profit. Saturn, a Tennessee plant in a right-to-work state with no union ties to speak of, would be a model of the future for the rest of the company to follow. Not! Lots of workers went there and came back dissatisfied. It's not for most of the rank and file. Lots of politics down there as well, from getting time off to getting the jobs they wanted, as they were all saddled with the new seniority date. No matter if they came from a different plant, they had to take what they got, and that was it. It took over a half billion dollars to start Saturn Corporation, and the employees of GM never received any money back from starting this company or thanks from the people of Tennessee for improving their quality of life. Not that we expected any. After all, we were GM. We always got the shaft. Some lawyer, some accountant, some judge, or some something of a politician would find a way into the pockets of the average working man or woman at GM. Saturn never really got off the ground. Marketing was not too good, and the product looked below average. Not to say that the product didn't have an impact. It did, but only on GM products. That plant produced higher-quality products at a cheaper price, and that is what GM was after. The price didn't come down, though. The bonuses just went up for the executives, as did the stock options. Stealing!

There was a new boss on the horizon—Stephen Yokich. He would resolve this matter for the rank and file. He did, kind of. He got us our raises, but left the quality network intact. More workers I'm sure he figured.were happy with the three percent raises. No more lump-sum raises at the end of the third quarter, but a nice raise that affected the whole package. Smart. One thing that he didn't get was the matching 401(k) proposal that I had put on the table for the rank and file. All the companies of the world were doing this to retain and keep workers, but I think that he gave this up to retain the numbers of the membership. The company always wanted to move to Mexico. Cheap labor. NAFTA is signed in 1993, but we have a contract, so the company must keep the work here for a while. Don't know what the politicians were thinking when they signed this law. Free trade. The problem is that there is no free commerce. The Mexican government doesn't care about us. The Canadian government will work with us, and always have, but they have national health care. The workers are paid in Canadian money, and the exchange favors them. NAFTA is not good for labor and not good for manufacturing in the U.S. When you lose manufacturing, you lose your tax base and the good-paying jobs that go along with it. Some of the politicians who signed this bill are still in office. Time to get them out and get new blood. No more thinking outside the box. It had nothing to do with Republicans or Democrats. It has to do with the fact that they're letting this country go down the path of service. Make those in power more accountable.

Drugs and Alcohol:

In 1977, the favorite drug was marijuana. It was all over the place and readily available. People used to pass a joint on the line on second shift. That was 1978, when the people all knew each other. The older workers would bring a bottle in after lunch and you could have a drink. Most of the work was done by then, or at least was almost over.

Speed was another drug that was used to be more productive. I didn't know why, but on Thursdays and Fridays certain people would race through their production and be done by lunch. They had gotten a fix. This remained the norm for a number of years. I think most workers would agree that after lunch, workers were much less productive than they were in the morning. When the company took away the incentive to be productive by having a standard, they lost the effort of the working membership. Big company mistake. It used to be that when you achieved your production quota, you were done, and now they want you to work by the hour and forget the standard. Something is lost with that. Employees don't come to work with any ambition or drive. The company continued to raise production so that it was basically impossible to gain a break or gain an edge. The edge was to use the system of downtime and find something that might make you faster. The edge was cocaine. The membership turned to a drug that would make them faster and would keep them awake, especially on third shift. They made no mistakes; they were just faster, and now they could get a break. The company praised their efforts, not knowing that they were killing themselves. We were getting older, and the fact remained that we should have had better jobs by then. Were in our third decade, and the fact remained that we didn't have the jobs we should have had. We all had families, and to achieve the new numbers the company wanted, we needed an edge.

GM hadn't hired any young people in years, and we were still considered young people. Fools! Both the membership and the corporation, along with the union cooperation, had created a situation that needed to be corrected. This resulted in the buyouts!

They didn't buy me out, because they didn't offer it to the '77s or '78s. Remember the tale of politics: Lots of employees with '76 seniority and union reps who were in the international union. They were taking care of their buddies. I don't want to hear "it is all we could do." I know better.

Offsites:

My first offsite job was in 1985 at Coldwater Road. They painted a picture of what would be the future of the auto industry. They said that the auto industry would be in transition. Most of us didn't believe it. They said that the Japanese would continue to make inroads and that the domestics would lose market share. It happened!

I went to many offsites during my career at GM. They never painted a picture of positivity. They almost resolved to become less of a company. They always wanted the membership to step up and do more while the corporation executives continued to take ridiculous bonuses. Antagonistic! The last offsite I went to was at Baker College, and the quality network people were there, putting it on. Get the picture. They were all trying to secure their jobs and not doing what they were supposed to do. These people have had these jobs for years, appointed or not. They're just hanging on till they can retire. You can change the top, but if you still have the same people receiving the message, then you will only go so far. Remember the Quality Network program. It began as a desperate attempt to help a company in need. Twenty plus years later, we find out it didn't work. The result: Retire everybody and start over.

Reinvent yourself. Bring back the cars that we remember. Don't wait till it is too late. The X and Y generations and my kids only know of the failures and the vans and the best trucks in the world. What happens if they don't want a truck? The discount isn't enough to make them buy GM. After all, GM isn't just an American company. It's just where they made their fortune!

Dirty Laundry: 1-7-85

Explaining the 1-7-85 date isn't as simple as any people think. It has to do with your original hire in date and is intended to protect the members of each individual plant from being overtaken by the unfortunate workers who were displaced from a different plant. Most GM workers got hired in to their respective plants in the '70s. The year 1984 was a transitional year for GM, with Roger Smith announcing closures and consolidations of facilities. The union had to do something. They did. They first created area hire pools and they also created the 1-7-85 area hire pool that most of us area hires got saddled with. We despised it. After all, we hired into GM on a certain date, and that is the date according to which we would get paid our vacation pay and our retirement. We had two dates: the one we hired in with at GM and then the 1-7-85 date we got saddled with. The only difference is that if our plant closed, then we got to take our seniority with us if our jobs went to this plant. Still confused? Don't be; we all had to learn the ropes, and then we found out that we didn't qualify for a particular job and we got stuck in a particular group. I was a welder for seventeen years. Some say this was because of choice, but because it was a closed group they would only allow some few workers out at a time. Due to my 1-7-85 seniority date, I couldn't get out. I tried to get out several times, but I learned that I would end up on a different shift, so I changed my mind. I finally took the risk when I knew I had no choice. Within the next few months, they would be cutting welders and I would be forced to move to a different classification. Welding jobs were being eliminated, and there was going to be a loss of jobs in the plant.

Vacation was always a piece of cake when I was a welder, but as soon as I became a truck driver, I wouldn't be able to get the time off I needed due to the 1-7-85 seniority date. I was low seniority now, even though I had twenty-eight years in at GM.

GM needed the drivers, and I was lowseniority.. We had to work when told, and overtime was always available. The welding group had taught me to forget about overtime.

I had gotten off the third week of July off during the previous four years, but the next year, my boss turned me down because I didn't have enough time. The funny thing was that I hadn't had to ask him during my last year because I was already off.

TRA Money:

The year was 1981, I think, and it was late fall when President Reagan signed a bill giving displaced workers some added cash for being laid off due to the ongoing trade deficit with Japan. Gas was at an all-time high at $1.19 per gallon, and the economy was in distress. Auto workers were getting laid off at a record pace, and the country was in a tailspin. It was my first real layoff that was indefinite, which meant there would be no recall date. I remember getting the check for a whopping 3,725 dollars. This was to cover time off during the previous year and also for the effects of the economy on the displaced workers. I was very excited when I received this money, and I thought we would be okay. I talked with my wife and decided that we would buy a house. We took the money that we got and put it together with the TRA money and the income tax money that I received from working for part of the year. We put $7,000 down on our first home. We bought it for $32,000 in Owosso. It was a beauty with three bedrooms and a bath and a half. It had a large kitchen, a basement with a shower, a two-bay garage, and a fenced-in lot for the dog. Great! Not so fast!

What! A few months later, I got a letter regarding the TRA money from the union. I thought they wanted their cut. No! They wanted the money! All of it, with the exception of a few hundred dollars. Of course, that would be upon my return to GM. They offered to take the money in increments of thirty or fifty dollars per week, whichever I agreed to. I didn't know that when I got federal monies that the union would ask for the money, claiming that I needed to pay the subfund back. I paid into the subfund while I worked, and then they took as many as five credits per week when the subfund was getting thin.

This was done to protect the workers with twenty years. Remember, the year was 1982 or early 1983. So much for the government helping out the little guy. If you didn't go back to GM, then you didn't have to pay back the union. Some members got as much as 10,000 dollars and never returned to GM. They had no tax penalty—no nothing—and of course, no union dues. Another opportunity was lost for the union and the workers.

I went back to work, and as you can imagine, we were only on a forty-hour schedule. Hey, they were taking money and union dues from me the first week I was back. Ridiculous. This was thirty to fifty bucks a week after tax, I might add. We owed the union and they as much as told us so. They were why we kept our good job. I didn't get to deduct the money off my income tax, either. After about a year, the union decided to get their money more quickly, and if you owed anything more, then you would pay fifty bucks per week until you were paid up. After that, they decided to go to one hundred bucks a week. Do you see any greed! They shouldn't have gotten a dime. I don't know how they did it, but they deducted the amount until you were paid up. I ended up in the hole and living on a couple of credit cards because of this due to the fact that I now was working for 35 percent less. I still paid two hours' worth of union dues per month, and I didn't mind doing that. The TRA money should have been mine and not the union's. I'm sure most of us remember those tough years. Owen Bieber was the union president, and he's the one who said he wouldn't go back and negotiate a contract after the membership turned down his two-year concession contract. What was he thinking? He made the rank and file suffer and take less for his own gratification and then he wanted to be remembered as a union president who stood up. Ha! The international union is nothing more than a clique, and if you win, you want to get in; and if you lose, then you're done. Especially at the local level. You have to suck a lot of hind end if you know what I mean. The international union has their own caucus, and they are never opposed, because if they are, and then you get beaten, you might as well forget it. You're blackballed. Greed! Politics! It's not what you know, but who you b----! You get the picture. All the union officials on the local level wanted to go into the international union. Why? Well I found out that they get an additional pension from the international union once they establish ten years of service. Of course, they also get a pension from GM. Two pensions! Yet they want the membership to take concessions. That is crazy. The rich get richer. They also want you to vote for their candidates. Why? They say it's because they are for the working man, but if you read between the lines, then you believe there must be more to it. The union never liked President Reagan, but I think the majority of the membership voted for him because he was good for the country, and he was. His death was the biggest funeral since J.F.K.'s. He was a giant among men. I finally paid off the TRA money to the union in 1984, and that is when the 401(k) went into effect and I could put a few bucks away for a rainy day. I did. I figured that I was making it without the thirty to fifty bucks a week, so why should I not try to do it before taxes. I wasn't the best investor, but I was not the worst either. I've done okay

Threatened!

It doesn't matter where you are; it just matters when the situation occurs. Especially at work, where you trying to do you best to make ends meet and bring home the bacon. You find people who feel comfortable creating drama and perhaps even causing chaos. These people have no reason to do this except that they are jealous and without confidence. They lack the drive and ability to overcome situations without venting out at someone, and the someone is you. You try to respect their thoughts, but when they turn ugly, whether they are racist or derogatory, it touches a nerve, and the rational side goes out the window. I've been called a honky, a suckass, a loser, a cocky bastard, and a bastard of hell. In each instance, these things happened because I did something that was different and out of the ordinary. I never followed the path of the norm. I enjoyed testing people, and I guess I deserved it. When you push people's buttons, you get different responses. I've always defended myself, but sometimes I'm outmatched. I can't fight against a gun and I can't fight against someone who won't compromise. I've always believed that you can change things, whatever they are, with enough pressure. Pressure causes people to react differently. Some choose violence, some choose activism, and some choose not to participate. You can only be one of the ones mentioned.

I am one to act. I never did like the fact that the union was a reactionary institution. They always waited till the membership was in bad shape to react to the situation. They had no plan and no vision for the future. They chose the low road. We have been threatened since the invasion of the Japanese companies on our soil in the '80s. The union should have organized them then. They didn't. They tried, but not hard enough. Where was the Ruether? They didn't pursue. Never quit. I still don't understand why their membership didn't want the representation. I guess they thought they had it pretty good. Guess what? They haven't faced retirement like the people of Delphi have. I thought they owed me something after thirty years, and I found out that their company might not make it. Scary! The fact is that people will do anything when cornered, and that is what the situation in the auto industry is today, thanks to the politics of it all and the fact that our representatives don't have the courage to defend our country and the way of life for the middle class. It doesn't matter whether they are Democrat or Republican; they both are at fault. Too bad we can't buy them out. All I know is that they think they are unbeatable, but change is inevitable. Pass the baton. Vote for the vision of the future; vote for an American-minded candidate.

Diversity:

What is it, and how can I fit in? It's the in thing these days. Creating diversity in the workplace or on campuses across the country these days is the buzz. Really! If you were a part of the '70s or even the '80s, you can relate to the fact of diversity. It is called affirmative action. Without affirmative action, you wouldn't have the kind of impact that this means today. We all want to be treated fairly and honestly; people do not want to get jobs because of race. They want to know that they are deserving and worthy of their positions and that race wasn't a deciding factor in their being hired. It might be a bonus, just like the fact that if you are a veteran, you get bonus points toward getting a federal job—post office included. Nonetheless, the fact remains that the pressure to promote or even hire someone of color has had an impact. If that isn't enough, when you throw gender into the equation, you have a real fiasco. Men and women are different and they know it. Some people are leaders and some are producers and followers. It doesn't mean that they don't have what it takes, but more or less they choose to have a different approach to life. They choose to be more relaxed and more satisfied with their happiness. I am one to pick up the ax and chop till I get what I want. I can be satisfied. I came to the conclusion that I wasn't going to be an artist or a leader just because it didn't happen when I expected it to.

Find Yourself:

It doesn't matter if you're the best flipper of hamburgers or the bet interior designer; it matters if you find yourself. If you can be happy with what you do, that is what you should be. Not all of us were meant to be graduate students or meant to be in the classroom. Some of us want to sing, and some of us want to dream. Dream of what you want and go for it. Opportunity knocks at your door. Don't settle for the ordinary. The world needs people like you. God made you special, and that is the truth, and whatever you want to be you can be. Well, maybe you can't be a millionaire without earning it, and that also might not be all it is cracked up to be, as it involves commitment, responsibility, and above all, the fact that you must trust people to do what is right with your money. Stress! I am one to opt out of the stress. I prefer to be comfortable, and as long as the world still goes around and my family is secure, I will be happy. I've been around, and I like what I see. The future is bright. Our youth will succeed us and deliver much greater things than we have done, and I'm proud to be a part of it. The real diversity is the inability of the older to let go and the young to grasp. The debt has been paid.

Leonard D. Lindquist

Last Thing To Say Before I Go Off to the Retirement World. Ha!

I just watched a conversation on *On the Money* on CNN. It is January 18, 2007. They were talking about where the UAW needs to go and how many concessions they were going to have to make in the next go-around during the upcoming negotiations. I think they forgot that they UAW just took a major hit in their numbers this month. 30,000 plus retired. When you're getting over fifty-six bucks a month from each of us and then it's gone, that seems a little ridiculous. The commentators think that the membership should just be happy to have jobs. These are people who never put on a welding helmet in 105-degree heat or been loaded with welding gear for eight hours while trying to not only make production, but also to do it right the first time. Neither have they had occasional sparks catch them in the exposed area of their necks. At seven hundred degrees Fahrenheit, it doesn't bleed; it just goes as far as it can go into the skin and scalds. This happens not once, but many times over the course of the years. You had better be covered up, or you could get caught with a sharp object in the arm and cut your arm wide open. Hey, no need for thirty-minute breaks; let's make it twenty-four, then twenty, then sixteen. It's a world economy. These jobs that we were running were already making money, but the greed factor came into play. Just a few more parts and then we could be global. GM already is global.

When I see the executives strap on a helmet for one day, or even one hour, then I'll feel that they will understand the effort that the men and women of the UAW have put forth for years. My father was one of the white-collar workers who would ask what I did. Even he didn't imagine the kind of effort that I put forward day in and day out to provide for my family. I'm rooting for a breakthrough in the political arena and in the heads of the corporation gurus, and for peace for the remaining workers. We should be entitled to a raise; we are no different from a teacher or an executive. We don't get stock options, we don't get bonuses, and we sure don't get profit sharing checks. This story that the world is changing is true, and yet it is still much the same. The price of vehicles hasn't gone down. Because we took concessions, only the pockets of the stockholders and executives have gotten fatter. How much more is ten million than nine million? Almost all of us who may have dreamed of being millionaires realize that this dream is for only the elite few who may have been lucky enough to be in the right place at the right time or who got the right promotion at the right time or whose stock took off at just the right time. It's timing. The UAW opened the door for the few to become the many. It allowed the government to provide many more programs with additional tax dollars. It allowed the private sector to grow and prosper in the American way. Restaurants were successful, and they spurred growth. Suppliers of everything you could think of sprung up. You say it was the '50's, but hey, it was the '70s that created the entire franchise boom in restaurants like Arby's and Burger King, and Bob Evans and their eggs and sausage with grits. World class means you don't take a back seat to anybody in quality, style, taste, or smiles. You pay your people well, and they tell others.

To me and to many, the GM V-8 is without question the best motor going, but the 3.8 liter V-6 that was built was the longest lasting V-6 in history. It was built by GM workers at the old Buick city plant. What a run. I salute those workers who were very dedicated. When you couldn't get a V-8, then you wanted the 3.8. It's not the workers or the workers' salaries that are killing the industry, but the much-applauded bean counters on Wall Street. You don't have to make 20 percent on everything to be successful. How about a 6- to

8-percent return. Almost everybody would be happy if the results would stay stable in that range. We all dream of more, but we would like some structure to our lives. After all, the stockbrokers then would have found something to do other than pick on the unions. If you listen closely, you will hear that the people have had enough. Not all of us will follow your path to the destruction of the U.S. manufacturing base and soon the destruction of our tax base. Some people will pull their money from the market altogether. Maybe the 401(k) will soon be the only way for people to have a retirement. Guess what; it's not. There's real estate and there is gold and there is antiques and all kinds of other things. Maybe paper money isn't worth as much as the stock brokers say it's worth, and just maybe the companies they say are worth so much are just like Enron. Maybe the people will start questioning the judgment of these people who keep putting the American worker down. Start questioning the politicians, your stock broker, and even your neighbor. Are those dollar stores really helping you out that much? When you're done with something, you just get rid of it and buy another. Fill the waste dumps with Chinese crap? Remember, Wal-mart used to stock only American products when Sam was the boss. He was proud of it. It was the cheapest place in town, but that was because he chose to sell cheaper. In the best interest of America, please make wise choices. Support those who support you.

The Final Word!

When you look back at all we have accomplished for the working families of the country, to see it broken down by some idea that we can do it better elsewhere is just ridiculous. My wife mentioned to me just yesterday that I didn't have a trade when I left, but that I was trained by the older workers. That is true. Not all of us are made for college. So why does everybody think they have to go, and why does the government push so many of the young that way? I hear the railroad is going to hire some 60,000 more workers to replace their aging workforce. They don't seem too concerned about the fact that they have to train the new hires. In fact, we should take a lesson from them. Trains don't need as much oil, and we would be less dependent on oil if we used more common transportation. We don't need so many truckers on the road. Unionize and be strong like it used to be. It might cost the big corporations more, but so what? I heard that the average CEO makes four hundred times the wage of the average workers he is trying to eliminate. The Lee Iacocca days are gone. I know he made his share, and good for him, but he also braved the storm and wasn't afraid to take a risk on the American worker. Let me get back to the fact that we all aren't made to go to school—I mean college. In fact, if you asked many of the high school graduates if they could get a job making fifteen to eighteen bucks an hour with the possibility to learn a trade with benefits like health care and the opportunity to become independent, they would gladly take the chance. There are always bumps in the road. You have just read it. What goes around comes around, and I think the American people have finally had enough of the politics and the taxes. Speaking of taxes, everybody should pay taxes. What! Well, not the people on Social Security, but the working class. I don't care if you make $10,000 or $1,000,000, you should pay something. Let's call it 10 percent of what you make. If you can find enough deductions to justify paying 10 percent, then you've done a good job. This business of paying nothing or having our debt in this country go through the roof is ridiculous. No matter what, you should pay your fair share. Hey, you don't have to close the loopholes, just know that when it's tax time, you're going to have to pay at least 10 percent whether you made any money or not. If you didn't make any money, then shame on you. You also should be a happy, cheerful giver. I mean, the Old Newsboys dedicate one day to raise money for the needy kids of their neighborhood, and you need to give generously. Give to your church or your family or your neighbor. You can't take it with you. I have excellent neighbors. They can fend for themselves, but some people can't. Shit happens! Either the loss of a job or loss of a family member can occur; you need to give generously. Talk to them. Life is too short to run and hide or go looking for something to do. It can wait. Take a breath. In closing, I wish for all the CEOs of this great country of ours to take notice. Think of what you've done in the last twelve to eighteen months and ask yourselves if that is what you want to leave as your legacy. Sure, you've made money in this country, but what have you given back? Give not only back to the community, but also to your company. Find some common ground with the rest of us. Walk every plant; touch every person who has made an impact on your life to make it better. Thank them, but most of all tell them that you have made a place for their children to work. Americans are competitive. We are the best in the world, give us a fair chance. Our political policies are in shambles. From NAFTA to CAFTA to other trade policies that haven't worked, the American worker deserves better. Elect better politicians. No particular party is right or wrong, but I will say this: You can't support anybody who doesn't support the American way of life. That means clearly the right to free speech and the right to free religion, but mostly the opportunity to earn a respectable living without help from the government. The government should also uphold the ability of the people to have a decent wage and retirement benefits. If you think that the young people can afford to put $2,000 away every year for forty years, then you're looking in a crystal ball. It's not going to happen. It's a great idea on paper. Paper doesn't pay the bills. This is especially true at sixty-five or sixty-seven or whatever the government decides is the normal age for retirement. We might be living longer, but in what type of environment? How many of us will end up in a nursing home at seventy-five?. We will have no money and no one who can support us. Our children won't be able to due to the global economy. That is not the American way. Elect new people who have vision! It's been a great ride, and I'm hopeful that our young people will rise up and fight to have the same benefits we have enjoyed. God bless.

Leonard Lindquist